Angular 19 for Beginners: A Step-by-Step Guide to Modern Web Development

James A. Velazquez

Copyright © 2025 James A. Velazquez

Contents

Introduction 6

Chapter 1: Your Angular Journey Begins 9

1.1 What is Angular? Unpacking the Power of this Web Framework 9

1.2 Single Page Applications (SPAs) Explained: The Secret Sauce Behind Modern Web Experiences 11

1.3 Navigating the Angular Ecosystem: Your Toolkit for Success 14

1.4 Essential Concepts: Components, Templates, and Data Binding - The Heart of Angular 18

Chapter 2: Setting Up Your Development Environment - Preparing for Liftoff! 23

2.1 Installing Node.js and npm: Laying the Cornerstone for Your Angular Projects 23

2.2 Installing the Angular CLI: Unleashing the Power of Command-Line Magic .. 26

2.3 Choosing a Code Editor: Selecting Your Digital Workshop 30

2.4 Basic Editor Configuration: Crafting Your Ideal Coding Environment 34

Chapter 3: Creating Your First Angular Application - Hello, Angular! 38

3.1 Using the Angular CLI: ng new - Laying the Foundation for Your Angular World 38

3.2 Project Structure Explained: Navigating Your Angular Labyrinth 42

3.3 Running Your Application: ng serve - Witnessing Your Angular Creation Come to Life 46

3.4 Exploring the Default App: Unpacking the Building Blocks 49

Chapter 4: Components: The Building Blocks - Assembling Your Angular Creations 55

4.1 What is a Component? The Cornerstone of Angular Architecture 55

4.2 Generating a New Component: ng generate component - Your Instant Component Factory 59

4.3 Component Anatomy: TypeScript, HTML, CSS - The Foundation of Every Angular Component 62

4.4 Displaying Data with Interpolation: The Simplest Path to Dynamic Content. 66

Chapter 5: Mastering Data Binding - Forging the Dynamic Connection 70

5.1 Interpolation: Displaying Values - Your First Brushstroke on the Angular Canvas 70

5.2 Property Binding: Setting Element Properties - Shaping the DOM Dynamically 74

5.3 Event Binding: Responding to User Actions - Building Truly Interactive Experiences 77

5.4 Two-Way Binding: [(ngModel)] for Input Fields - The Magic of Synchronization 81

5.5 Building a Simple Counter: A Data Binding Symphony in Action 85

Chapter 6: Directives: Adding Logic to Templates - Empowering Your HTML.......... 90

6.1 What are Directives? Giving HTML Superpowers 91

6.2 *ngIf: Conditional Rendering - Controlling Visibility with Precision 94

6.3 *ngFor: Looping Through Data - The Key to Dynamic Collections 98

6.4 [ngClass]: Dynamic CSS Classes - Shaping the View with Style 102

6.5 [ngStyle]: Dynamic Inline Styles - Direct Manipulation of Visual Appearance 106

6.6 Example: Styling a List - A Symphony of Directives 109

Chapter 7: Pipes: Transforming Data - Polishing Your Data Presentation 114

7.1 What are Pipes? - Data Transformation for Elegant Presentation 114

7.2 DatePipe: Formatting Dates - A Timeless Transformation 117

7.3 CurrencyPipe: Formatting Currencies - Making Monetary Values Understandable 121

7.4 UpperCasePipe and LowerCasePipe: Text Case - Enforcing Consistent Style 124

7.5 Custom Pipes (Basic Introduction) - Your Personalized Data Transformation Toolkit 127

Chapter 8: User Input and Forms - Gathering Information and Interacting with Users 132

8.1 Template-Driven Forms: An Overview - The Fast Track to Form Handling... 133

8.2 Binding Inputs: ngModel in Action - Establishing the Two-Way Connection136

8.3 Handling Form Submission: Capturing and Processing User Data 139

8.4 Basic Form Validation: Guarding the Gates of Data Integrity 142

8.5 Building a Contact Form: A Symphony of User Interaction........................... 146

Chapter 9: Component Communication - Building a Harmonious Ecosystem........ 153

9.1 @Input(): Passing Data to Child Components - The One-Way Flow of Information 153

9.2 @Output(): Emitting Events from Child Components - Signaling Action Upwards 157

9.3 Building a Reusable Card Component: A Symphony of Communication and Design... 161

Chapter 10: Project: Build a To-Do List App - A Practical Synthesis of Angular Skills 167

10.1 Project Requirements: Charting the Course for Our To-Do List App.......... 167

10.2 Component and Service Structure: Building a Solid Architectural Foundation 171

10.3 Implementing the UI: Weaving the Visual Tapestry of Our Application 174

10.4 Adding Functionality: Breathing Life into Our Application 175

10.5 Styling the App: Adding the Final Touches of Elegance and Clarity........... 182

Chapter 11: Next Steps in Angular - Expanding Your Horizons 187

11.1 Introduction to Services and Dependency Injection (Conceptual): The Power of Reusable Logic 187

11.2 Introduction to Angular Routing: Mapping the User's Journey 190

11.3 Introduction to HTTP Communication: Connecting Your App to the Data Universe 194

11.4 Further Learning Resources: Equipping You for Continued Growth 197

11.5 Best Practices for Beginners: Navigating the Angular Landscape with Confidence 200

Appendix: Your Reference and Troubleshooting Guide 204

Introduction

Welcome! If you're picking up this book, you're likely curious about Angular – maybe you've heard about its power for building modern web applications, or perhaps you're looking for a framework to structure your web development projects. Whatever your reason, you've come to the right place. This book is designed to take you from complete beginner to someone who can confidently build real-world applications with Angular 19.

Let's be honest: learning a new framework can feel daunting. There's a lot to take in, and it's easy to get lost in jargon and complex concepts. That's why this book takes a step-by-step approach, breaking down Angular into manageable pieces. Think of it as learning to play a musical instrument – we'll start with the basic chords and gradually work our way up to more complex melodies.

Who This Book Is For

This book is specifically written for individuals who are new to Angular and may even be new to web development in general. If any of the following describe you, you're in the right place:

- **Absolute Beginners:** You've never used Angular before, or perhaps you've only dabbled a little.
- **Frontend Developers Looking to Learn Angular:** You're familiar with HTML, CSS, and JavaScript, and you want to add Angular to your skillset.
- **Career Changers:** You're looking to enter the world of web development and want to learn a popular and in-demand framework.
- **Students:** You're learning web development as part of your studies and need a practical guide to Angular.

Don't worry if you don't have a deep understanding of every web development concept. We'll explain everything you need to know along the way.

What You Will Learn

By the end of this book, you'll be able to:

- **Set up your Angular development environment:** Install the necessary tools and configure your code editor.
- **Understand Angular fundamentals:** Grasp the core concepts of components, templates, data binding, directives, and pipes.
- **Build interactive user interfaces:** Create dynamic web pages that respond to user actions.
- **Work with forms and user input:** Collect data from users and validate their input.
- **Communicate between components:** Pass data and events between different parts of your application.
- **Build a complete application:** Create a working to-do list application from scratch.
- **Understand the next steps:** Know where to go to continue learning Angular and explore more advanced topics.

You'll learn through clear explanations, real-world examples, and hands-on exercises. We'll provide complete, working code examples that you can copy and paste into your own projects. We'll also highlight common mistakes and provide tips for troubleshooting.

Why Angular?

So, why choose Angular? In a world of many JavaScript frameworks, Angular stands out for several reasons:

- **Structured Development:** Angular provides a clear structure for building large, complex applications. This makes your code more organized, maintainable, and scalable.
- **Component-Based Architecture:** Angular's component-based architecture allows you to create reusable UI elements, making development faster and more efficient.
- **TypeScript:** Angular uses TypeScript, a superset of JavaScript that adds static typing and other features that improve code quality and developer productivity.
- **Powerful CLI:** The Angular CLI (Command Line Interface) makes it easy to create new projects, generate components, and perform other common tasks.
- **Large and Active Community:** Angular has a large and active community of developers who contribute to the framework and provide support.
- **Backed by Google:** Angular is developed and maintained by Google, ensuring its long-term stability and evolution.

Personally, I've found that Angular's structured approach helps me stay organized, especially on larger projects. And the TypeScript support has significantly reduced the number of runtime errors I encounter. While there's definitely a learning curve, the payoff in terms of productivity and maintainability is well worth it.

Ready to embark on your Angular journey? Let's dive in!

Chapter 1: Your Angular Journey Begins

Welcome to the first step of your Angular adventure! In this chapter, we'll lay the groundwork for your understanding of Angular. We'll answer the fundamental question: "What *is* Angular?" and explore the concepts that make it so powerful. Think of this chapter as your roadmap – it'll help you understand where we're going and why. Don't worry if everything doesn't click immediately. We'll revisit these concepts throughout the book.

1.1 What is Angular? Unpacking the Power of this Web Framework

Let's get straight to the point: Angular is a robust and popular framework for building sophisticated web applications. But what *exactly* does that entail? It's not just a simple library you plug into your HTML; it's a comprehensive toolkit and a structured philosophy for web development. Think of it as a complete workshop with all the necessary tools, instructions, and even some pre-built components to get you started building a complex machine.

Angular: More Than Just a Library

Many JavaScript libraries exist, but Angular is more than that. It's a **framework**. This distinction is crucial. A library is a collection of helpful functions that you call when you need them. You're in charge of how and when to use them. A framework, on the other hand, provides a structure and a set of rules for building your application. It dictates how your code should be organized and how different parts of your application should interact.

Why is this structure important?

- **Consistency:** Angular provides a consistent way to build applications, making it easier for developers to collaborate and maintain code over time. Everyone knows where things are and how they should work.
- **Scalability:** With its structured architecture, Angular makes it easier to build large, complex applications that can scale to meet growing demands. As your application grows, the framework helps keep things organized.

- **Maintainability:** A well-structured Angular application is easier to maintain and update, reducing the risk of introducing bugs and making it easier to add new features.

Angular's Core Strengths: Building Dynamic Experiences

The primary focus of Angular is building **dynamic web applications.** "Dynamic" means that the content on the page can change without requiring a full page reload. This results in a much smoother and more responsive user experience.

Think about your favorite social media site. When you scroll down, new posts load automatically without the page flashing or reloading. That's the kind of dynamic behavior that Angular excels at creating.

This dynamic nature is essential for modern web applications because users expect a seamless and responsive experience. They don't want to wait for pages to reload every time they interact with the site.

Key Features that Power Angular's Capabilities:

- **Component-Based Architecture:** The foundation of Angular is its component-based architecture. This means that your application is built from reusable UI elements called components. Each component encapsulates its own logic, template (HTML), and styling (CSS). This makes your code modular, testable, and easy to maintain. We'll explore components in detail in later chapters.
- **Data Binding:** Angular provides a powerful data binding mechanism that automatically synchronizes data between your component's logic and the HTML template. This means that when the data changes in your component, the template is automatically updated, and vice versa. This simplifies the process of displaying and updating data in your application. We'll explore data binding in depth as well.
- **Dependency Injection:** Angular has a robust dependency injection system that allows you to easily manage the dependencies between different parts of your application. This makes your code more testable and reusable. Don't worry if this sounds complicated now; we'll cover it in detail later.
- **TypeScript:** Angular is written in TypeScript, a superset of JavaScript that adds static typing and other features. TypeScript helps you catch errors early in the development process and makes your

code more maintainable. If you haven't used TypeScript before, don't worry; we'll introduce you to it gradually.

Personal Insight: When I first started using Angular, I was initially intimidated by the framework's complexity. However, once I understood the core concepts, I realized how much more efficient and organized it made my development process. The component-based architecture and data binding features, in particular, significantly reduced the amount of code I had to write and made it easier to maintain my applications.

Why Google's Backing Matters

Angular is developed and maintained by Google. This has several important implications:

- **Long-Term Stability:** You can be confident that Angular will continue to be developed and supported for the foreseeable future. Google is committed to the framework and invests significant resources in its development.
- **Continuous Improvement:** Google is constantly working to improve Angular, adding new features and optimizing performance. This ensures that Angular remains a cutting-edge framework.
- **Large Community:** Angular has a large and active community of developers who contribute to the framework and provide support. This means that you'll have plenty of resources available if you need help.

In essence, Angular is a comprehensive framework that provides the tools and structure you need to build modern, dynamic web applications. It's a powerful tool that can significantly improve your productivity and the quality of your code. While there's a learning curve, the rewards are well worth the effort.

1.2 Single Page Applications (SPAs) Explained: The Secret Sauce Behind Modern Web Experiences

We've established that Angular is great for building dynamic web applications. A huge part of that is because it empowers you to create something called a **Single Page Application**, or SPA. But what *is* an SPA, and why is it such a big deal? Let's unravel this concept and see why it's central to the modern web.

The Traditional Web: A Page-by-Page Journey

To really understand SPAs, it's helpful to contrast them with how traditional websites work. Imagine browsing a classic website. Every time you click a link – navigating to a new page, submitting a form, or even just changing a filter – your browser sends a request to the server. The server processes that request and sends back an entirely new HTML page.

This process works, of course, but it has some drawbacks:

- **Full Page Reloads:** The browser has to re-download all the assets (HTML, CSS, JavaScript, images) for each new page. This can be slow and create a jarring user experience, with the page flashing and re-rendering.
- **Server Load:** Every page request puts a load on the server, which can become a problem with high traffic.

SPAs: One Page to Rule Them All

Single Page Applications take a different approach. As the name suggests, an SPA loads **a single HTML page** when you first visit the website. After that, *all* subsequent interactions – clicking links, submitting forms, updating data – are handled dynamically by JavaScript *within that single page.*

Think of it like this: you're setting up a stage once and then changing the scenery, props, and actors as needed, without ever having to rebuild the entire stage.

How SPAs Work: The Key Components

1. **Initial Load:** The browser sends a request to the server, and the server sends back the initial HTML page, along with the necessary CSS and JavaScript. This initial load might take a bit longer than a traditional website.
2. **Client-Side Routing:** Instead of the server handling navigation, the SPA uses JavaScript to manage routing on the *client-side* (in the browser). When you click a link, the JavaScript code updates the URL and displays the appropriate content, without requesting a new page from the server.
3. **Dynamic Content Updates:** The SPA uses JavaScript to fetch data from a backend API and dynamically update the content on the page. This can involve fetching data in JSON format and using JavaScript

to manipulate the DOM (Document Object Model) – the structure of the HTML page.

4. **Backend API:** SPAs typically rely on a separate backend API to provide data and handle server-side logic. The API exposes endpoints that the SPA can use to fetch and update data.

Benefits of SPAs: A Smoother, Faster Experience

The SPA approach offers several significant advantages:

- **Improved User Experience (UX):** SPAs provide a much smoother and more responsive user experience because they avoid full page reloads. The transitions between different parts of the application are seamless and instantaneous.
- **Faster Loading Times:** After the initial load, subsequent updates are much faster because the browser only needs to download data, not entire HTML pages.
- **Reduced Server Load:** Because SPAs handle routing and content updates on the client-side, they reduce the load on the server.
- **Offline Capabilities:** SPAs can be designed to work offline by caching data and assets in the browser.
- **Mobile-Friendly:** SPAs are well-suited for mobile devices because they can provide a native-like app experience.

Examples of SPAs: Familiar Faces

You're likely using SPAs every day without even realizing it! Here are some popular examples:

- **Gmail:** The entire email interface updates dynamically without page reloads.
- **Google Maps:** Navigating the map, searching for locations, and viewing details all happen within a single page.
- **Facebook/Twitter:** Scrolling through your feed, posting updates, and interacting with content all occur without full page reloads.
- **Netflix/Spotify:** Browsing movies/music, playing content, and managing your account are all handled within a single page.

Personal Insight: I remember the first time I used a properly built SPA. It felt magical! The responsiveness and fluidity of the application were a game-changer. It completely transformed my expectations for web applications.

Why Angular and SPAs Are a Perfect Match

Angular is designed specifically for building SPAs. It provides a robust framework for managing routing, data binding, and component communication, making it easier to create complex and interactive single-page applications. Angular provides features like:

- **Angular Router:** Angular's built-in router allows you to easily define routes and navigate between different parts of your application.
- **Data Binding:** Angular's data binding features make it easy to display data in your template and update the data when the user interacts with the UI.
- **Component-Based Architecture:** Angular's component-based architecture allows you to create reusable UI elements, which simplifies the development of large SPAs.

In a Nutshell:

SPAs are a fundamental part of modern web development. They provide a smoother, faster, and more engaging user experience. Angular is a powerful framework that makes it easier to build complex and sophisticated SPAs.

1.3 Navigating the Angular Ecosystem: Your Toolkit for Success

Learning Angular isn't just about mastering the framework itself; it's also about understanding the tools and technologies that surround it. Think of it as becoming a skilled carpenter. You need to know how to use the hammer and saw, but you also need to understand the different types of wood, the importance of measuring accurately, and the best ways to join pieces together. Similarly, understanding the Angular ecosystem will make you a more effective and efficient Angular developer.

Beyond Angular: A Collaborative Environment

The Angular ecosystem is a collection of tools, libraries, and practices that work together to streamline the development process. It's not just one monolithic thing; it's a collaborative environment designed to make building complex web applications easier and more efficient.

Let's explore the essential components:

- **The Angular CLI (Command Line Interface): Your Command Center**

  The Angular CLI is arguably the most important tool in the Angular ecosystem. It's a command-line tool that automates many common tasks, making development faster and less error-prone.

  Think of the CLI as your personal assistant, handling repetitive tasks so you can focus on the creative aspects of development.

  Key CLI Features:

  - **Project Creation (ng new):** Creates a new Angular project with a pre-configured structure and essential dependencies. This sets you up for success from the very beginning.
  - **Component Generation (ng generate component):** Creates new components with the necessary files and boilerplate code. This saves you time and ensures consistency across your project.
  - **Service Generation (ng generate service):** Creates new services for managing data and logic.
  - **Module Generation (ng generate module):** Creates new modules for organizing your application into logical units.
  - **Build and Serve (ng build, ng serve):** Builds your application for production and serves it locally for development.
  - **Testing (ng test, ng e2e):** Runs unit tests and end-to-end tests to ensure the quality of your code.

  Example: To create a new Angular project named "my-app", you would simply run the following command in your terminal:

  ```
  ng new my-app
  ```

  The CLI will then prompt you for some configuration options (e.g., whether to use routing and which stylesheet format to use) and create the project structure for you.

- **TypeScript: Adding Structure and Safety to JavaScript**

Angular is built with TypeScript, a superset of JavaScript that adds static typing and other features. While you can write Angular code in plain JavaScript, TypeScript is the recommended approach for several reasons:

o **Early Error Detection:** TypeScript helps you catch errors during development, before you even run your code. This can save you a lot of time and frustration.

o **Improved Code Readability:** TypeScript's static typing makes your code easier to understand and maintain, especially for large projects.

o **Better Code Completion:** TypeScript provides better code completion and refactoring tools in your code editor.

Think of TypeScript as adding guardrails to your JavaScript code, helping you avoid common pitfalls and making your code more robust.

- **npm, yarn, or pnpm: Managing Your Project's Dependencies**

npm (Node Package Manager), yarn, and pnpm are package managers that allow you to easily install and manage dependencies (libraries and tools) for your Angular project. Dependencies are external pieces of code that your project relies on to function.

For instance, you might use a third-party library for charting, date formatting, or making HTTP requests. Package managers make it easy to install, update, and remove these dependencies.

Example: To install the popular charting library Chart.js using npm, you would run the following command:

```
npm install chart.js
```

This command will download Chart.js and its dependencies and add them to your project.

- **RxJS (Reactive Extensions for JavaScript): Handling Asynchronous Operations**

RxJS is a library for working with asynchronous data streams and events. It provides a powerful way to handle complex asynchronous operations, such as HTTP requests and user interactions.

While RxJS can seem intimidating at first, it's an essential part of Angular, especially when dealing with data from backend APIs.

We'll cover RxJS in more detail later in the book, but for now, just know that it's a powerful tool for managing asynchronous data.

- **Component Libraries: Accelerating UI Development**

Several component libraries provide pre-built UI components that you can use in your Angular applications. These libraries can save you a lot of time and effort in styling and implementing common UI elements, such as buttons, forms, dialogs, and grids.

Some popular Angular component libraries include:

  - **Angular Material:** Google's official component library for Angular, providing a set of Material Design components.
  - **PrimeNG:** A rich set of UI components with a wide range of features.
  - **NG-Bootstrap:** A library providing Bootstrap components for Angular.

These libraries provide you with pre-built, tested, and styled components, allowing you to focus on the unique aspects of your application rather than reinventing the wheel.

- **Testing Frameworks: Ensuring Code Quality**

Testing is an essential part of the Angular development process. Several testing frameworks are available to help you write unit tests and end-to-end tests for your code.

  - **Jasmine:** A popular testing framework that provides a set of tools for writing unit tests.
  - **Karma:** A test runner that executes your unit tests in a browser.
  - **Protractor:** A testing framework for writing end-to-end tests, simulating user interactions with your application.

17

Testing helps you ensure the quality of your code and prevent

1.4 Essential Concepts: Components, Templates, and Data Binding- The Heart of Angular

If Angular were a body, then Components, Templates, and Data Binding would be its heart, lungs, and circulatory system. These three concepts are fundamental to understanding how Angular works and how to build dynamic web applications. Mastering these will set you on a strong path to Angular proficiency. Let's explore each in detail, relating them to real-world scenarios to make them easier to grasp.

Components: Reusable Building Blocks

Imagine you're building with LEGOs. Each LEGO brick is a self-contained unit with a specific shape and function. You can combine these bricks in various ways to create larger structures. In Angular, **components** are like those LEGO bricks.

What is an Angular Component?

An Angular component is a self-contained, reusable unit of code that encapsulates the logic, template (HTML), and styling (CSS) for a specific part of the user interface. Each component is responsible for rendering a specific section of the page and handling user interactions within that section.

Key Characteristics of Components:

- **Encapsulation:** A component encapsulates its own data, logic, and styling, preventing it from interfering with other parts of the application.
- **Reusability:** Components can be reused throughout the application, saving you time and effort in writing code.
- **Modularity:** Components promote modularity by breaking down the application into smaller, manageable units.
- **Testability:** Components are easier to test because they are self-contained and have well-defined interfaces.

Real-World Examples of Components:

- **Navigation Bar:** A component displaying navigation links and user login information.
- **Product Card:** A component displaying information about a single product (image, title, price, description).
- **Comment Section:** A component displaying a list of comments and allowing users to add new comments.
- **Login Form:** A component allowing users to enter their username and password.

Creating a Simple Component

In Angular, a component typically consists of three parts:

1. **TypeScript Class:** Contains the component's logic, data, and methods.
2. **HTML Template:** Defines the structure and content of the component's view.
3. **CSS Stylesheet:** Defines the styling for the component's view.

We'll delve into creating components in more detail later, but here's a simple example:

```
// my-component.component.ts
import { Component } from '@angular/core';

@Component({
  selector: 'app-my-component', // How we reference this component in HTML
  templateUrl: './my-component.component.html', // The HTML template
  styleUrls: ['./my-component.component.css']   // The CSS styles
})
export class MyComponent {
  title = 'Hello from MyComponent!';
}

    <!-- my-component.component.html -->
<h1>{{ title }}</h1>
```

In this example, MyComponent has a title property, which is displayed in the HTML template.

Templates: Defining the View

The **template** of a component is simply an HTML file that defines the structure and content of the component's view. It's where you specify what the user will see on the screen. Templates can contain HTML elements, Angular directives, data binding expressions, and other elements that dynamically render content.

What Can Templates Do?

Templates can:

- Display data from the component using interpolation ({{ }}).
- Bind properties of HTML elements to data in the component using property binding ([property]="value").
- Respond to user events using event binding ((event)="handler()").
- Conditionally render content using directives like *ngIf.
- Loop through data and display it using directives like *ngFor.

Templates are where the visual magic happens, transforming data into a user-friendly interface.

Data Binding: Bridging Logic and View

Data binding is the glue that connects your component's TypeScript code (the logic) with its HTML template (the view). It's a mechanism that automatically synchronizes data between the component and the template, ensuring that the view always reflects the current state of the component's data.

Types of Data Binding in Angular:

- **Interpolation:** Displays data from the component in the template. For example: <h1>{{ title }}</h1>. This displays the value of the title property in an <h1> tag.
- **Property Binding:** Binds a property of an HTML element to a data value in the component. For example: <img [src]="imageUrl">. This sets the src attribute of the <img> tag to the value of the imageUrl property.
- **Event Binding:** Binds an event (e.g., click, mouseover) to a method in the component. For example: <button (click)="handleClick()">Click Me</button>. This calls the handleClick() method when the button is clicked.

- **Two-Way Binding:** Allows you to both display and update data in the template. For example: <input [(ngModel)]="name">. This binds the value of the <input> element to the name property in the component, so that when the user types in the input field, the name property is automatically updated, and vice versa.

Personal Insight: Data binding was a revelation for me when I first encountered it. Before, I was manually updating the DOM using JavaScript, which was tedious and error-prone. Data binding automated this process, making it much easier to build dynamic user interfaces.

Putting It All Together: The Synergy of Components, Templates, and Data Binding

These three concepts work together seamlessly to create dynamic Angular applications:

1. **The component** holds the data and logic.
2. **The template** defines the structure and layout of the view.
3. **Data binding** connects the data in the component to the template, ensuring that the view always reflects the current state of the data.

Mastering these three concepts is essential for becoming a proficient Angular developer. In subsequent chapters, we'll explore each of these concepts in more detail and provide practical examples of how to use them to build real-world applications. For now, focus on understanding the basic principles.

Summary

In this chapter, you've taken your first steps on your Angular journey. We've defined what Angular is, explored the concept of SPAs, introduced the Angular ecosystem, and touched on the essential concepts of components, templates, and data binding.

Don't feel pressured to memorize everything right away. The goal is to familiarize yourself with these concepts so that you can build upon them in the following chapters. In the next chapter, we'll get our hands dirty and set up our development environment, so we can start building our first Angular application!

Key Takeaways:

- Angular is a framework for building dynamic web applications.
- SPAs provide a smoother user experience.
- The Angular ecosystem includes tools like the CLI, TypeScript, and npm.
- Components, templates, and data binding are essential concepts in Angular.

Ready to move on to Chapter 2 and set up your development environment? We'll put these concepts into practice very soon!

Chapter 2: Setting Up Your Development Environment - Preparing for Liftoff!

Before we can start building amazing Angular applications, we need to set up our development environment. Think of this as preparing your workshop before you start a woodworking project. You need the right tools, a clean workspace, and a clear understanding of how everything works. Don't worry, it's not as complicated as it sounds! We'll walk through each step together. By the end of this chapter, you'll have a fully configured environment ready for Angular development.

2.1 Installing Node.js and npm: Laying the Cornerstone for Your Angular Projects

Before we can even *think* about writing Angular code, we need to establish a solid foundation. That foundation is Node.js and npm (Node Package Manager). These two are intertwined and absolutely essential for modern web development, particularly when working with frameworks like Angular. Think of Node.js and npm as the cement and tools that bind all the other pieces together.

Why Node.js? Stepping Outside the Browser

Historically, JavaScript lived solely within the confines of web browsers. Node.js changed everything. It's a **JavaScript runtime environment** that allows you to execute JavaScript code *outside* the browser. This means you can use JavaScript to build server-side applications, command-line tools, and, in our case, powerful development tools like the Angular CLI.

The Significance of a Runtime Environment:

A runtime environment provides the necessary resources and libraries to execute code written in a specific programming language. Node.js provides the libraries and tools needed to run JavaScript code on your computer, just like a browser does.

Why is Node.js important for Angular?

- **Running the Angular CLI:** As we've mentioned, the Angular CLI is built with Node.js. You need Node.js to run the CLI commands that create projects, generate components, and build your application.
- **Building and Serving Your Application:** Node.js is used to build your Angular application for production and to serve it locally for development.
- **Running Development Servers:** Many Angular development workflows rely on Node.js-based development servers to automatically reload your application when you make changes to the code.

npm: Managing the Ecosystem

npm (Node Package Manager) is the default package manager for Node.js. It's a vast online repository of open-source JavaScript packages (libraries, tools, and frameworks) that you can easily install and manage in your projects.

Think of npm as a giant online store for JavaScript code. You can find almost anything you need, from UI components to utility libraries, and install them with a single command.

Why is npm important for Angular?

- **Installing Dependencies:** Angular projects rely on numerous dependencies, such as the Angular framework itself, third-party libraries, and development tools. npm makes it easy to install, update, and remove these dependencies.
- **Managing Dependencies:** npm keeps track of all the dependencies in your project and their versions, ensuring that your application works correctly.
- **Publishing Packages:** You can also use npm to publish your own packages, making them available to other developers in the community.

Alternatives to npm:

While npm is the most widely used package manager for Node.js, alternatives like **yarn** and **pnpm** offer some performance and security advantages. However, for beginners, npm is the recommended starting point due to its simplicity and widespread adoption. We'll stick with npm in this book.

Step-by-Step Installation Guide: Getting Node.js and npm on Your System

1. **Download Node.js:** Visit the official Node.js website (https://nodejs.org/) and download the installer for your operating system (Windows, macOS, or Linux).

   Important: Choose the **LTS (Long Term Support)** version. The LTS version is generally more stable and recommended for beginners. The "Current" version may have newer features but may also be less stable.

2. **Run the Installer:** Run the downloaded installer and follow the on-screen instructions.

   Crucial Step (Windows Users): During the installation, make sure you **check the box that says "Add to PATH."** This will automatically add Node.js to your system's PATH environment variable, allowing you to run node and npm commands from any directory in your terminal.

3. **Verify Installation:** Open a new terminal window (or command prompt) on your system.

   Run the following commands to verify that Node.js and npm are installed correctly:

   ```
   node -v
   npm -v
   ```

   If you see version numbers displayed for both Node.js and npm, congratulations! You've successfully installed them.

Troubleshooting Common Issues:

- **Permission Errors:** If you encounter permission errors during the installation process, especially on macOS or Linux, try running the installer or the npm install command with administrator privileges using sudo.

  ```
  sudo npm install -g @angular/cli
  ```

25

- **node or npm Commands Not Recognized:** If you try to run node or npm commands and get an error message saying that the commands are not recognized, it means that Node.js is not added to your PATH environment variable.
  - **Windows:** Restart your computer. This will often resolve the issue. If not, you may need to manually add Node.js to your PATH environment variable. Search online for instructions specific to your Windows version.
  - **macOS/Linux:** Make sure your terminal is configured to load your shell profile (e.g., .bash_profile, .zshrc). You may need to restart your terminal or source your profile.

Personal Insight: I remember struggling with PATH variables when I first started learning web development. It seemed like a black box. Don't be afraid to Google it! Understanding PATH variables is a valuable skill that will save you a lot of headaches down the road.

Conclusion: A Solid Foundation

Installing Node.js and npm is a critical first step in your Angular journey. These tools provide the foundation for building and managing your Angular projects. By following the steps outlined in this section, you've laid the cornerstone for your Angular development. Now, you're ready to move on to the next step: installing the Angular CLI.

2.2 Installing the Angular CLI: Unleashing the Power of Command-Line Magic

Now that we have Node.js and npm set up, it's time to install the Angular CLI (Command Line Interface). This is *the* tool you'll be using constantly throughout your Angular development journey. Think of it as your magic wand, allowing you to conjure up new projects, components, services, and much more with simple commands. The CLI drastically simplifies the development process, letting you focus on building features rather than wrestling with boilerplate code.

What is the Angular CLI?

The Angular CLI is a command-line interface that automates many common tasks in Angular development. It's a powerful tool that simplifies project creation, code generation, building, testing, and deployment. It helps enforce best practices and provides a consistent structure across your projects.

Why is the Angular CLI so important?

- **Project Scaffolding:** The CLI makes it incredibly easy to create new Angular projects with a pre-configured structure and essential dependencies. It sets you up for success from the very beginning.
- **Code Generation:** The CLI can generate components, services, modules, directives, and pipes with a single command. This saves you a lot of time and effort in writing boilerplate code.
- **Build Automation:** The CLI automates the process of building your Angular application for production, optimizing it for performance and creating deployable packages.
- **Testing:** The CLI makes it easy to run unit tests and end-to-end tests to ensure the quality of your code.
- **Deployment:** The CLI can help you deploy your Angular application to various hosting providers.

In essence, the Angular CLI is like a Swiss Army knife for Angular development. It's a versatile tool that can handle a wide range of tasks, making your development process faster, more efficient, and less error-prone.

Global vs. Local Installation:

You can install the Angular CLI globally or locally.

- **Global Installation (Recommended for Beginners):** Installing the CLI globally allows you to use it from any directory on your system. This is the recommended approach for beginners because it's simpler to set up.
- **Local Installation:** Installing the CLI locally installs it only within a specific project. This is useful for managing different versions of the CLI for different projects. However, it requires more configuration and is generally not recommended for beginners.

We'll focus on the global installation in this book, as it's the easiest way to get started.

Step-by-Step Installation Guide: Installing the Angular CLI Globally

1. **Open a Terminal Window:** Open a new terminal window (or command prompt) on your system.
2. **Install the Angular CLI Globally:** Run the following command to install the Angular CLI globally:

```
npm install -g @angular/cli
```

Explanation:

- npm install: This is the npm command for installing packages.
- -g: This flag tells npm to install the package globally.
- @angular/cli: This is the name of the Angular CLI package. The @angular prefix indicates that it's an official Angular package.

The installation process may take a few minutes, depending on your internet connection and computer speed.

3. **Verify Installation:** After the installation is complete, run the following command to verify that the Angular CLI is installed correctly:

```
ng version
```

Explanation:

- ng: This is the command for invoking the Angular CLI.
- version: This option tells the CLI to display its version information.

If you see version information for the Angular CLI, congratulations! You've successfully installed it.

Troubleshooting Common Issues:

- **Permission Errors:** As with Node.js, you may encounter permission errors during the installation process, especially on macOS or Linux.

If this happens, try running the command with administrator privileges using sudo.

```
sudo npm install -g @angular/cli
```

- **ng Command Not Recognized:** If you try to run the ng command and get an error message saying that the command is not recognized, it means that npm's global packages directory is not added to your PATH environment variable.
  - **Windows:** Restart your computer. This will often resolve the issue. If not, you may need to manually add npm's global packages directory to your PATH environment variable. Search online for instructions specific to your Windows version.
  - **macOS/Linux:** Make sure your terminal is configured to load your shell profile (e.g., .bash_profile, .zshrc). You may need to restart your terminal or source your profile.

Personal Insight: When I first started using the Angular CLI, I was amazed at how much time it saved me. Before, I had to manually create all the files and folders for a new component, which was tedious and time-consuming. The CLI automated this process, allowing me to focus on writing the actual component logic.

A Word About Different Versions:

Angular evolves quickly, and new versions are released regularly. It's important to keep your Angular CLI and your project's Angular dependencies up to date to take advantage of the latest features and bug fixes.

The CLI makes it easy to update your Angular projects to the latest version. We'll cover updating Angular projects later in the book.

Conclusion: You're Ready to Roll!

Installing the Angular CLI is a crucial step in setting up your Angular development environment. With the CLI installed, you can now create new projects, generate code, and build your applications with ease. You're well on your way to becoming an Angular pro!

2.3 Choosing a Code Editor: Selecting Your Digital Workshop

Now that we have the foundational tools installed (Node.js, npm, Angular CLI), let's turn our attention to your primary workspace: your code editor. Think of your code editor as your digital workshop where you'll be spending countless hours crafting your Angular masterpieces. Choosing the right editor can significantly impact your productivity, enjoyment, and overall development experience.

More Than Just a Text Editor:

A code editor is much more than just a place to write code. A good code editor provides a range of features that make coding easier, faster, and less error-prone.

Key Features to Look For:

- **Syntax Highlighting:** Displays code in different colors and styles to make it easier to read and understand.
- **Code Completion (IntelliSense):** Suggests code snippets and function names as you type, saving you time and reducing typos.
- **Error Checking (Linting):** Checks your code for errors and style violations in real-time, helping you catch bugs early.
- **Debugging:** Provides tools for debugging your code, allowing you to step through the code, inspect variables, and identify the root cause of errors.
- **Refactoring:** Provides tools for refactoring your code, making it easier to rename variables, extract functions, and perform other code transformations.
- **Version Control Integration:** Integrates with version control systems like Git, allowing you to easily commit changes, branch code, and collaborate with other developers.
- **Extensibility:** Supports extensions that add new features and functionality.

The Contenders: Popular Code Editors for Angular Development

There's no single "best" code editor; the ideal choice depends on your personal preferences, budget, and specific needs. However, here are some of the most popular and highly recommended code editors for Angular development:

- **Visual Studio Code (VS Code): The Free Powerhouse**

  Developed by Microsoft, Visual Studio Code (VS Code) is a free, open-source code editor that has become incredibly popular among web developers. It's a lightweight but powerful editor that offers a wide range of features, excellent TypeScript support, and a vast ecosystem of extensions.

  Key Advantages of VS Code:

  - **Free and Open-Source:** It's completely free to use and open-source, making it accessible to everyone.
  - **Excellent TypeScript Support:** VS Code has excellent built-in support for TypeScript, including syntax highlighting, code completion, and error checking.
  - **Large Ecosystem of Extensions:** VS Code has a vast ecosystem of extensions that add new features and functionality, such as support for Angular-specific tools, linting, formatting, and debugging.
  - **Built-in Git Integration:** VS Code has built-in support for Git, making it easy to commit changes, branch code, and collaborate with other developers.
  - **Integrated Terminal:** VS Code has an integrated terminal, allowing you to run commands directly from the editor.

  Personal Recommendation: VS Code is my personal favorite code editor for Angular development, and it's what I'll be using throughout this book. It's a great choice for both beginners and experienced developers.

- **WebStorm: The Commercial IDE**

  WebStorm is a commercial IDE (Integrated Development Environment) developed by JetBrains, the company behind popular IDEs like IntelliJ IDEA and PyCharm. WebStorm is a powerful and feature-rich IDE specifically designed for web development.

  Key Advantages of WebStorm:

- **Comprehensive Feature Set:** WebStorm offers a comprehensive set of features, including advanced code completion, refactoring tools, debugging, and testing support.
- **Excellent JavaScript and TypeScript Support:** WebStorm has excellent support for JavaScript and TypeScript, including advanced code analysis and refactoring tools.
- **Integration with Other JetBrains Tools:** WebStorm integrates seamlessly with other JetBrains tools, such as IntelliJ IDEA and PyCharm.

Considerations: WebStorm is a commercial product, so you'll need to purchase a license to use it. However, it's a worthwhile investment for serious developers who want a powerful and feature-rich IDE.

- **Sublime Text: The Speed Demon**

Sublime Text is a popular text editor known for its speed, simplicity, and extensibility. It's a lightweight editor that's great for working with code quickly.

Key Advantages of Sublime Text:

- **Speed and Performance:** Sublime Text is known for its speed and performance, even when working with large files.
- **Extensibility:** Sublime Text has a large ecosystem of plugins that add new features and functionality.
- **Cross-Platform Support:** Sublime Text is available for Windows, macOS, and Linux.

Considerations: Sublime Text is a commercial product, but you can use it for free indefinitely, although you'll occasionally see a prompt to purchase a license.

- **Atom: The Hackable Editor**

Atom is a free, open-source code editor developed by GitHub. It's a highly customizable editor that's known for its extensibility.

Key Advantages of Atom:

- **Free and Open-Source:** It's completely free to use and open-source.

- o **Highly Customizable:** Atom is highly customizable, allowing you to tailor it to your specific needs and preferences.
- o **Large Community:** Atom has a large community of users, so you can easily find help and resources online.

Considerations: Atom can be slower than some other editors, especially when working with large projects.

A Quick Comparison Table:

Feature	VS Code	WebStorm	Sublime Text	Atom
Price	Free	Commercial	Commercial	Free
TypeScript	Excellent	Excellent	Good	Good
Extensibility	Excellent	Good	Excellent	Excellent
Performance	Good	Good	Excellent	Fair
Git Integration	Built-in	Built-in	Plugin	Plugin

Personal Insight: I've tried all of these editors at some point in my career, and while they all have their strengths, I always come back to VS Code. Its combination of features, performance, and extensibility makes it the perfect fit for my workflow.

Making Your Choice: Try Before You Buy (or Don't Buy!)

The best way to choose a code editor is to try out a few different ones and see which one you like the best. Most code editors offer free trials or free versions, so you can experiment before committing to a purchase.

Don't be afraid to switch editors if you find that your initial choice isn't working out for you. It's a personal decision, and you should choose the tool that makes you the most productive and happy.

Conclusion: Your Code Editor Awaits

Choosing a code editor is an important step in setting up your Angular development environment. The right editor can make coding more enjoyable, efficient, and less error-prone. Take the time to explore different options and find the editor that's right for you. Now, let's move on to configuring that editor for optimal Angular development!

2.4 Basic Editor Configuration: Crafting Your Ideal Coding Environment

Choosing your code editor is only half the battle. Once you've picked the right tool, you need to configure it to optimize it for Angular development. Think of this as customizing your workshop layout, organizing your tools, and setting up the lighting just right. A well-configured editor can significantly boost your productivity and make coding a more enjoyable experience.

Why Configuration Matters:

Out of the box, most code editors offer basic functionality. However, configuring your editor with the right settings and extensions can unlock a whole new level of productivity.

Essential Configuration Steps:

1. **Install Essential Extensions:** Extensions are add-ons that enhance your code editor with new features and functionality. Here are some must-have extensions for Angular development:
   - **Angular Language Service:** Provides advanced code completion, error checking, and refactoring tools for Angular templates and TypeScript code. This is arguably the *most important* extension.
   - **ESLint:** A JavaScript/TypeScript linter that checks your code for errors and style violations.
   - **Prettier:** A code formatter that automatically formats your code to a consistent style.
   - **TSLint (Deprecated, but still useful for older projects):** A TypeScript linter that checks your code for errors and style violations. Note that TSLint is being deprecated in favor of ESLint.
   - **EditorConfig for VS Code:** Helps maintain consistent coding styles across different editors and projects.
   - **Bracket Pair Colorizer:** Colorizes matching bracket pairs, making it easier to see the structure of your code.
   - **Auto Rename Tag:** Automatically renames matching HTML/XML tags.

- o **GitLens:** Supercharges the Git capabilities built into VS Code.
2. **Configure TypeScript Settings:** TypeScript is the primary language for Angular development, so it's important to configure your code editor to work well with TypeScript.
    - o **Enable Automatic Type Checking:** Make sure your editor is configured to automatically check your TypeScript code for type errors. This will help you catch errors early in the development process.
    - o **Configure TypeScript Version:** Specify the version of TypeScript you want to use for your projects.
3. **Set Up Linting and Formatting:** Linting and formatting tools help you maintain a consistent coding style and prevent errors.
    - o **Install ESLint and Prettier:** Install ESLint and Prettier as development dependencies in your project:

```
npm install --save-dev eslint prettier eslint-plugin-prettier eslint-config-prettier
```

- o **Configure ESLint:** Create an ESLint configuration file (.eslintrc.js or .eslintrc.json) in your project root and configure it to use the recommended Angular ESLint rules. There are many guides online for this.
    - o **Configure Prettier:** Create a Prettier configuration file (.prettierrc.js or .prettierrc.json) in your project root and configure it to your preferred style.
    - o **Integrate with Your Editor:** Install the ESLint and Prettier extensions in your code editor and configure them to automatically lint and format your code on save.
4. **Customize Keybindings:** Keybindings are keyboard shortcuts that allow you to perform common tasks quickly. Customize the keybindings in your code editor to match your preferences and workflow.
    - o **Common Keybinding Customizations:**
        - Format Code: Set a keybinding for formatting your code with Prettier.
        - Save All: Set a keybinding for saving all open files.
        - Toggle Terminal: Set a keybinding for toggling the integrated terminal.
5. **Adjust Editor Appearance:** Customize the appearance of your code editor to make it more visually appealing and easier to read.

- o **Choose a Theme:** Select a theme that you find visually appealing and easy on the eyes. There are many themes available for most code editors.
- o **Adjust Font Size and Family:** Adjust the font size and family to make the code more readable.
- o **Enable Word Wrap:** Enable word wrap to prevent long lines of code from extending beyond the visible area.

Specific Configuration for VS Code (Example):

Let's walk through some specific configuration steps for VS Code:

1. **Install Essential Extensions:**
   - o Open VS Code.
   - o Click on the Extensions icon in the Activity Bar (or press Ctrl+Shift+X).
   - o Search for and install the following extensions:
     - Angular Language Service
     - ESLint
     - Prettier - Code formatter
     - EditorConfig for VS Code
     - Bracket Pair Colorizer
     - Auto Rename Tag
     - GitLens
2. **Configure ESLint and Prettier:**
   - o Follow the instructions in the ESLint and Prettier documentation to configure them in your project. This typically involves creating configuration files (.eslintrc.js, .prettierrc.js) and adding them to your project root.
3. **Customize Keybindings:**
   - o Open the Keyboard Shortcuts settings (File -> Preferences -> Keyboard Shortcuts or Code -> Preferences -> Keyboard Shortcuts).
   - o Search for the commands you want to customize (e.g., "Format Document", "Save All", "Toggle Integrated Terminal").
   - o Click on the pencil icon next to the command and enter your desired keybinding.
4. **Adjust Editor Appearance:**
   - o Open the Settings (File -> Preferences -> Settings or Code -> Preferences -> Settings).

o   Search for the settings you want to adjust (e.g.,
    "editor.fontSize", "editor.fontFamily", "editor.wordWrap").
o   Enter your desired values in the settings.

Personal Insight: I used to think that configuring my code editor was a waste of time, but I quickly realized that it was one of the best investments I could make. A well-configured editor can save you hours of time each week and make coding a much more enjoyable experience.

Important Tip: Don't be afraid to experiment with different settings and extensions to find what works best for you. There's no one-size-fits-all approach to code editor configuration.

Conclusion: Your Personalized Coding Oasis

Configuring your code editor is an essential step in setting up your Angular development environment. By installing the right extensions, configuring TypeScript settings, setting up linting and formatting, customizing keybindings, and adjusting the editor appearance, you can create a personalized coding oasis that maximizes your productivity and enjoyment. Now, you're truly ready to dive into the world of Angular development!

Chapter 3: Creating Your First Angular Application - Hello, Angular!

With our development environment set up and our code editor configured, it's time for the fun part: creating your first Angular application! This chapter will guide you through the process of creating a new Angular project using the Angular CLI, exploring the project structure, running the application, and taking a peek at the default app that Angular generates for you. Think of this as your "Hello, World!" moment in Angular.

3.1 Using the Angular CLI: ng new- Laying the Foundation for Your Angular World

So, you've got your tools ready, you've got your coding workspace prepped, and you're itching to build something with Angular. That's fantastic! Now it's time to summon our magical assistant – the Angular CLI – and use the ng new command to conjure a brand new Angular project into existence.

ng new: More Than Just a Project Creator

The ng new command is your starting point for every Angular project. But it's not just a simple "create folder" command. It's a sophisticated project initializer that does the following:

- **Scaffolds a Complete Project Structure:** The CLI generates a well-organized project structure that follows Angular best practices. This includes folders for components, services, assets, and more.
- **Installs Essential Dependencies:** It automatically installs all the necessary dependencies for your project, including the Angular framework itself, RxJS, TypeScript, and other essential libraries.
- **Configures the Project:** It sets up the necessary configuration files, such as angular.json, package.json, and tsconfig.json, which control how your project is built, tested, and deployed.
- **Initializes Git (Optional):** It can optionally initialize a Git repository for your project, making it easy to track changes and collaborate with other developers.

Why is ng new so important?

Before the Angular CLI, setting up a new Angular project was a tedious and error-prone process. You had to manually create all the folders, install the dependencies, and configure the project. This was time-consuming and required a deep understanding of Angular's inner workings.

ng new automates all of these steps, ensuring that your project is set up correctly from the very beginning. It also enforces best practices and provides a consistent structure across your projects. This makes it easier to collaborate with other developers and maintain your code over time.

Step-by-Step Guide: Creating a New Angular Project with ng new

1. **Open a Terminal Window:** Open a new terminal window (or command prompt) on your system.
2. **Navigate to Your Development Directory:** Use the cd command to navigate to the directory where you want to create your Angular project. This is where the project folder will be created. A common practice is to have a dev or projects folder within your Documents directory. For example:

```
cd Documents/dev
```

3. **Run the ng new Command:** Run the following command to create a new Angular project:

```
ng new my-first-app
```

   Explanation:

   - ng new: This is the Angular CLI command for creating a new project.
   - my-first-app: This is the name of your project. Choose a descriptive name. Use lowercase letters and hyphens to separate words (e.g., my-ecommerce-app, angular-blog).
4. **Answer the Prompts:** The CLI will interactively guide you through setting up some basic project options. These prompts are important because they affect the initial configuration of your app. Let's look at them individually:

- o **"Would you like to add Angular routing?"**
  - **Yes:** If you answer "Yes," the CLI will configure your project to use Angular's built-in routing module. Routing allows you to navigate between different views or pages within your application. For single-page applications, routing is essential.
  - **No:** If you answer "No," the CLI will not configure routing. You can always add it later, but it's generally easier to include it from the beginning.

  Recommendation: For most projects, especially anything beyond the simplest demo, **answer "Yes"** to this question.

- o **"Which stylesheet format would you like to use?"**

  The CLI will present you with several options for your project's stylesheet format:

  - **CSS:** The standard stylesheet format for the web.
  - **SCSS:** A superset of CSS that adds features like variables, nesting, and mixins. SCSS is very popular and offers more power and flexibility than plain CSS.
  - **Sass:** Another superset of CSS, similar to SCSS.
  - **Less:** A CSS preprocessor that provides features similar to SCSS and Sass.
  - **Stylus:** A CSS preprocessor that uses a more concise syntax than CSS, SCSS, or Less.

  Recommendation: For beginners, **CSS is a perfectly fine starting point**. It's the most widely understood. However, **SCSS is highly recommended for most projects** due to its added features and benefits. Sass is essentially the same as SCSS, but the syntax is slightly different. Less and Stylus are also good options, but less commonly used in the Angular community.

5. After you answer these questions, the CLI will start generating your project and installing the dependencies. This may take a few minutes, depending on your internet connection and computer speed. Be patient!
6. **Navigate to Your Project Directory:** Once the project is created, use the cd command to navigate to your project directory:

```
cd my-first-app
```

You are now inside your Angular project!

Troubleshooting Common Issues:

- **"Command Not Found: ng"**: This typically means that the Angular CLI is not installed globally or that your system's PATH environment variable is not configured correctly. Double-check the installation instructions in the previous chapter.
- **Slow Installation:** If the installation process is taking a long time, it may be due to a slow internet connection or a large number of dependencies being installed.
- **Errors During Installation:** If you encounter errors during the installation process, carefully read the error messages and try to resolve the issues. Common causes include:
    - Missing dependencies: Make sure you have Node.js and npm installed correctly.
    - Permission issues: Try running the command with administrator privileges.

Personal Insight: I remember the first time I used the ng new command. It felt like magic. I went from having nothing to a fully functional Angular project in just a few minutes. It was a huge productivity boost!

A Note on Customization:

The ng new command accepts several options that allow you to customize the project creation process. You can explore these options by running ng new --help. For example, you can use the --style option to specify the stylesheet format you want to use:

```
ng new my-app --style scss
```

Conclusion: Your Project is Born!

The ng new command is your key to unlocking the power of Angular. By using this command, you can quickly create new Angular projects with a well-organized structure and all the necessary dependencies. You're now ready to explore the project structure, run your application, and start building amazing things with Angular!

3.2 Project Structure Explained: Navigating Your Angular Labyrinth

You've successfully used the ng new command to create your first Angular project. Congratulations! Now, you're probably staring at a folder full of files and directories, wondering where to start. Don't worry; it's a common feeling. This section will be your guide to understanding the purpose of each key file and folder, giving you a clear roadmap for navigating your Angular project. Think of this as learning the layout of your new home - knowing where everything is will make you feel much more comfortable.

Why Understanding the Project Structure is Crucial

A well-structured project is easier to understand, maintain, and collaborate on. The Angular CLI generates a project structure that follows Angular best practices, making it easier to build scalable and maintainable applications.

Understanding the project structure will:

- **Help you find the files you need quickly.**
- **Make it easier to understand how different parts of the application fit together.**
- **Enable you to follow best practices for organizing your code.**
- **Facilitate collaboration with other developers.**

Let's take a tour of the key files and folders:

- **node_modules/ - The Land of Dependencies**

  This folder is like a hidden engine room containing all the external libraries and packages your project relies on. Don't meddle with it directly!

  o **What it contains:** All the dependencies for your project, including the Angular framework itself, RxJS, TypeScript, and third-party libraries.
  o **Why it's important:** Without these dependencies, your Angular application wouldn't be able to function.

- o **Key takeaway:** You typically don't need to modify anything in this folder directly. npm (or yarn/pnpm) manages this folder for you.
- o **Ignore it in Git (usually):** This folder is usually excluded from version control (Git) because it can be very large and is easily recreated using npm install. The .gitignore file handles this.

- **src/ - The Heart of Your Application**

  This is where all the *actual* code you write lives. Inside the src directory, you'll find the core components, services, modules, and assets that make up your Angular application. It's the creative center of your project.

  - o **app/ - Your Application's Core**

    This folder contains the main application module and the root component of your application. It's the starting point for your Angular application.

    - **app.component.ts:** The TypeScript file for the root component (AppComponent). This file defines the component's logic, data, and methods.
    - **app.component.html:** The HTML template for the root component. This file defines the structure and content of the component's view.
    - **app.component.css (or .scss, etc.):** The CSS stylesheet for the root component. This file defines the styling for the component's view.
    - **app.module.ts:** The TypeScript file for the main application module (AppModule). This module declares the components, services, and other modules used in your application.
  - o **assets/ - Static Resources**

    This folder is for static assets like images, fonts, and other files that don't need to be processed by the build system. These are resources your application uses directly.

  - o **environments/ - Configuration for Different Environments**

This folder contains environment-specific configuration files (e.g., environment.ts for development and environment.prod.ts for production). These files allow you to configure your application differently for different environments. This is extremely useful for things like API endpoints that differ between development and production.

- **index.html - The Entry Point**

  This is the main HTML file for your application. It's the file that's loaded when you visit your application in the browser. It's a very simple file that mainly just bootstraps the Angular application.

- **main.ts - The Bootstrapper**

  This is the entry point for your application. This file bootstraps the main application module (AppModule). This is where the Angular magic begins!

- **styles.css (or .scss, etc.) - Global Styles**

  This file contains the global styles for your application. You can define CSS rules here that apply to all components in your application.

- **angular.json - The Project's Blueprint**

This is *the* configuration file for your Angular project. It controls how your project is built, tested, and deployed. This is where you'll configure things like:

- **Build options:** Specify the build target, output path, and other build settings.
- **Test settings:** Configure the testing framework and test runner.
- **Deployment settings:** Specify the deployment target and deployment options.

Important: You don't usually need to edit this file manually, but it's important to understand its purpose. The CLI provides commands for managing most of the settings in this file.

- **package.json - The Project's Identity**

  This file contains metadata about your project, such as its name, version, description, dependencies, and scripts. It's used by npm to manage your project's dependencies and run various tasks. Key sections include:

  - dependencies: Lists the dependencies your application needs to run in production.
  - devDependencies: Lists the dependencies used for development, such as testing frameworks and linting tools.
  - scripts: Defines shortcuts for running common tasks, such as building, testing, and serving your application. For example, npm start typically runs ng serve.
- **tsconfig.json - TypeScript Configuration**

  This file contains the configuration settings for the TypeScript compiler. It specifies how your TypeScript code should be compiled into JavaScript.

  Why is TypeScript Configuration Important?

  TypeScript provides static typing and other features that improve code quality and developer productivity. The tsconfig.json file allows you to configure the TypeScript compiler to enforce these features and generate JavaScript code that is compatible with your target environment.

- **.gitignore - Ignoring the Unnecessary**

  This file specifies which files and folders should be ignored by Git (version control). This is important for excluding files that are not necessary for version control, such as the node_modules folder and build output files.

Personal Insight: When I first started using Angular, I was intimidated by the sheer number of files and folders in a new project. It took me some time to understand the purpose of each file and how they all fit together. But once I did, it made developing Angular applications much easier and more enjoyable.

Navigating with Confidence:

Understanding the project structure is essential for navigating your Angular labyrinth with confidence. By knowing where to find each file and folder, you'll be able to quickly locate the code you need, understand how different parts of the application fit together, and follow best practices for organizing your code. Now you're armed with the knowledge to confidently explore your project!

3.3 Running Your Application: ng serve- Witnessing Your Angular Creation Come to Life

You've successfully created your Angular project and explored its structure. Now comes the exciting part: bringing your application to life! The ng serve command is your key to doing just that. Think of ng serve as flipping the switch to power on your Angular creation.

ng serve: More Than Just a Server

ng serve does more than just start a local web server. It's a powerful command that automates several tasks, making development much easier and more efficient. It essentially does the following:

- **Builds Your Application:** It compiles your TypeScript code, processes your HTML templates, and bundles your CSS stylesheets into a set of optimized files that can be served by a web browser.
- **Starts a Development Server:** It starts a lightweight web server that serves your application from your local machine.
- **Watches for Changes:** It watches your project files for changes. When you save a file, it automatically rebuilds your application and refreshes your browser, allowing you to see your changes in real-time. This is often referred to as "hot reloading".
- **Provides Live Reloading:** It automatically reloads your browser whenever your application is rebuilt, so you don't have to manually refresh the page.

Why is ng serve so essential?

Before tools like ng serve, developers had to manually build their applications and deploy them to a web server every time they made a change. This was time-consuming and inefficient.

ng serve automates this process, allowing you to focus on writing code and seeing your changes in real-time. This makes development much faster, more iterative, and more enjoyable. The immediate feedback loop is invaluable.

Step-by-Step Guide: Running Your Angular Application with ng serve

1. **Open a Terminal Window:** Open a terminal window in your project directory. Make sure you're in the root directory of your Angular project (the one containing angular.json and package.json).
2. **Run the ng serve Command:** Run the following command to build and serve your application:

```
ng serve
```

   Explanation:

   o ng serve: This is the Angular CLI command for building and serving your application locally.

   The CLI will start building your application. You'll see a series of messages in the terminal window as the CLI compiles your code, processes your templates, and bundles your assets.

3. **Open Your Browser:** Once the build process is complete, the CLI will display a message indicating that the development server is listening on a specific port (usually http://localhost:4200).

   Open your web browser and navigate to the URL provided by the CLI (e.g., http://localhost:4200).

   You should see the default Angular application running in your browser. Congratulations! You've successfully run your Angular application using ng serve.

4. **Experiment and Observe Live Reloading:** Now, open any of the files in your project directory (e.g., src/app/app.component.html) and make a small change. For example, change the title property in app.component.ts and save the file.

You'll see the CLI automatically rebuild your application and your browser automatically refresh to reflect the changes you made. This is the power of live reloading in action!

Troubleshooting Common Issues:

- **"Port Already in Use" Error:** If you see an error message indicating that the port is already in use, it means that another application is already running on that port. You can resolve this by either stopping the other application or specifying a different port for ng serve using the --port option:

```
ng serve --port 4201
```

- **Build Errors:** If you encounter build errors, carefully read the error messages in the terminal window and try to resolve the issues. Common causes include:
  o Syntax errors in your code
  o Type errors in your TypeScript code
  o Missing dependencies
- **Application Not Loading in Browser:** If the application doesn't load in your browser, make sure the development server is running and that you're navigating to the correct URL. Also, check your browser's developer console for any error messages.

Advanced ng serve Options:

The ng serve command supports several options that allow you to customize its behavior. You can explore these options by running ng serve --help. Some useful options include:

- --open (or -o): Automatically opens your browser to the application URL when the server starts.

```
ng serve --open
```

- --host: Specifies the host address for the development server (e.g., --host 0.0.0.0 to make the server accessible from other devices on your network).

- --configuration: Specifies the configuration to use for building the application (e.g., --configuration production to use the production configuration).

Personal Insight: I still remember the days before live reloading. It was a pain to manually refresh the browser every time I made a change. ng serve has completely transformed my development workflow and made it much more enjoyable.

Conclusion: Witnessing Your Angular Creation Come Alive!

The ng serve command is your key to seeing your Angular application in action. By using this command, you can quickly build your application, start a development server, and watch for changes in real-time. You're now ready to explore the default app that Angular generates for you and start building your own amazing features!

3.4 Exploring the Default App: Unpacking the Building Blocks

You've successfully created your first Angular application and seen it running in your browser. Excellent! Now, it's time to peek under the hood and examine the code that makes up the default application. This section will dissect the key components of the default app, giving you a foundational understanding of how Angular applications are structured and how components, templates, and modules work together. Think of this as learning the anatomy of an Angular application – understanding the different parts and how they function together.

Why is exploring the default app important?

The default app generated by the Angular CLI is a great starting point for learning Angular. It provides a basic but functional application structure that you can use as a template for your own projects. By exploring the code in the default app, you can gain a better understanding of:

- **Component Structure:** How Angular components are organized and how they interact with each other.
- **Template Syntax:** How to use Angular's template syntax to display data and handle user interactions.

- **Module Organization:** How Angular modules are used to organize and modularize your application.
- **Dependency Injection:** How Angular's dependency injection system works.

Key Components of the Default App:

Let's break down the key files and components that make up the default app:

- **src/app/app.component.ts - The Root Component's Logic**

    This TypeScript file defines the logic for the root component of your application, AppComponent. It's the top-level component that serves as the container for all other components in your application.

```
import { Component } from '@angular/core';

@Component({
  selector: 'app-root',
  templateUrl: './app.component.html',
  styleUrls: ['./app.component.css']
})
export class AppComponent {
  title = 'my-first-app';
}
```

    Key Elements Explained:

    o import { Component } from '@angular/core';: This line imports the Component decorator from the @angular/core module. The Component decorator is used to mark a class as an Angular component.
    o @Component({ ... }): This is the Component decorator itself. It's used to configure the component with metadata such as its selector, template, and styles.
    o selector: 'app-root': This specifies the CSS selector that you can use to insert the component into the HTML. In this case, you can use the <app-root> tag in your index.html file to display the component.
    o templateUrl: './app.component.html': This specifies the path to the HTML template for the component.

- o styleUrls: ['./app.component.css']: This specifies the paths to the CSS stylesheets for the component. You can include multiple stylesheets.
- o export class AppComponent { ... }: This defines the AppComponent class, which contains the component's logic and data.
- o title = 'my-first-app';: This defines a property named title with the value 'my-first-app'. This property can be accessed in the component's template.

- **src/app/app.component.html - The Root Component's View**

This HTML file defines the template for the root component. It's where you specify what the user will see on the screen. This is where you use Angular's data binding syntax to display data from the component and handle user interactions. It usually contains other components and HTML elements.

The default template is automatically generated, so its content will vary depending on the Angular version you are using. It will usually have things like:

- o Interpolation ({{ }}): To display the component's title
- o Links: To official Angular documentation

- **src/app/app.component.css (or .scss, etc.) - Styling the Root Component**

This CSS file defines the styling for the root component. You can define CSS rules here that apply only to the elements in the component's template. This is how you control the visual appearance of the component.

- **src/app/app.module.ts - Organizing the Application**

This TypeScript file defines the main application module, AppModule. Modules are used to organize and modularize your Angular application.

```
import { BrowserModule } from '@angular/platform-browser';
import { NgModule } from '@angular/core';

import { AppComponent } from './app.component';
```

```
@NgModule({
  declarations: [
    AppComponent
  ],
  imports: [
    BrowserModule
  ],
  providers: [],
  bootstrap: [AppComponent]
})
export class AppModule { }
```

Key Elements Explained:

- o import { BrowserModule } from '@angular/platform-browser';: This line imports the BrowserModule from the @angular/platform-browser module. The BrowserModule provides essential services for running Angular applications in a web browser.
- o import { NgModule } from '@angular/core';: This line imports the NgModule decorator from the @angular/core module. The NgModule decorator is used to mark a class as an Angular module.
- o declarations: [AppComponent]: This specifies the components, directives, and pipes that belong to this module. In this case, it declares that the AppComponent belongs to the AppModule.
- o imports: [BrowserModule]: This specifies the other modules that this module depends on. In this case, it imports the BrowserModule.
- o providers: []: This specifies the services that are available to this module.
- o bootstrap: [AppComponent]: This specifies the component that should be bootstrapped when the application starts. In this case, it specifies that the AppComponent should be bootstrapped.
- **src/index.html - The HTML Entry Point**

This is the main HTML file for your application. It's the file that's loaded when you visit your application in the browser. It mainly just contains the <app-root> tag, which is used to insert the root component into the HTML.

```
    <!doctype html>
<html lang="en">
<head>
  <meta charset="utf-8">
  <title>MyFirstApp</title>
  <base href="/">

  <meta name="viewport" content="width=device-width, initial-
scale=1">
  <link rel="icon" type="image/x-icon" href="favicon.ico">
</head>
<body>
  <app-root></app-root>
</body>
</html>
```

Key Elements Explained:

- o <app-root></app-root>: This tag is used to insert the root
      component (AppComponent) into the HTML. The app-root
      selector is defined in the AppComponent class.
- **src/main.ts - Bootstrapping the App**

    This file contains the code that bootstraps the Angular application.
    It's the entry point that tells Angular to start running the application.

```
    import { enableProdMode } from '@angular/core';
import { platformBrowserDynamic } from '@angular/platform-
browser-dynamic';

import { AppModule } from './app/app.module';
import { environment } from './environments/environment';

if (environment.production) {
  enableProdMode();
}

platformBrowserDynamic().bootstrapModule(AppModule)
  .catch(err => console.error(err));
```

Key Elements Explained:

- o platformBrowserDynamic().bootstrapModule(AppModule):
      This line bootstraps the AppModule, starting the Angular
      application.

Personal Insight: I remember when I first started learning Angular, I was overwhelmed by all the different files and components. But once I started exploring the default app and understanding how everything fit together, it became much easier to build my own applications.

Putting It All Together: How the Pieces Connect

The default Angular app demonstrates the core concepts of Angular:

1. The AppModule declares and organizes the application's components.
2. The AppComponent is the root component that serves as the container for all other components.
3. The AppComponent has a template (app.component.html) that defines the structure and content of the view.
4. The main.ts file bootstraps the AppModule, starting the Angular application.
5. The index.html file loads the AppModule and displays the AppComponent in the browser.

By understanding how these pieces connect, you can start building your own amazing Angular applications!

Conclusion: You've Seen the Inner Workings!

Exploring the default Angular app is a crucial step in learning Angular. By dissecting the key components and understanding how they work together, you've gained a valuable foundation for building your own Angular applications. Now, you're ready to move on to Chapter 4 and start building your own components!

Chapter 4: Components: The Building Blocks - Assembling Your Angular Creations

Welcome to the heart of Angular! In this chapter, we're diving deep into the concept of **components**, which are the fundamental building blocks of all Angular applications. Think of components as the LEGO bricks you use to construct complex structures. Understanding components is absolutely essential for becoming a proficient Angular developer.

4.1 What is a Component? The Cornerstone of Angular Architecture

We're embarking on a deeper dive into the core concept of Angular: components. To truly master Angular, you must fundamentally understand components, as they're the linchpin of everything you'll build. More than just reusable bits of UI, they are the key to building maintainable, scalable, and testable Angular applications.

Beyond Reusability: The Essence of a Component

While reusability is a major benefit, the heart of a component lies in the concept of **encapsulation.** Encapsulation is the bundling of data (state) and methods (behavior) that operate on that data within a single unit, and restricting access to that unit's internal workings.

What does encapsulation mean in practice for Angular components?

- **Scoped Data:** Each component has its own private data, or *state*. This data is not directly accessible from other components, preventing accidental modification and promoting predictability. The component controls its own data.
- **Controlled Behavior:** A component defines the methods that can be used to interact with its data and update its view. This ensures that the component's behavior is consistent and predictable.
- **Isolated Styling:** Components can have their own CSS styles, which are scoped to that component. This prevents style conflicts with other

components and makes it easier to maintain the styling of your application. Components have their own visual presentation.

Why is encapsulation so important?

- **Maintainability:** Encapsulation makes it easier to maintain your code because changes to one component are less likely to affect other components. This reduces the risk of introducing bugs when you update your application.
- **Testability:** Encapsulated components are easier to test because you can test them in isolation, without having to worry about their interactions with other parts of the application.
- **Reusability:** Encapsulation makes components more reusable because they don't depend on the specific context in which they are used. You can use a component in different parts of your application without having to modify its code.

Component Anatomy: A Closer Look

Let's illustrate this with a concrete example. Imagine we're building a shopping application and need to display product information. We can create a ProductCardComponent to display each product's name, description, image, and price.

Conceptual View of a ProductCardComponent:

```
+-----------------------------------------+
| ProductCardComponent                    |
+-----------------------------------------+
| Private Data:                           |
|    - productName: string                |
|    - productDescription: string         |
|    - productPrice: number               |
|    - productImage: string               |
+-----------------------------------------+
| Public Methods (API):                   |
|    - addToCart(): void                   |
|    - viewDetails(): void                |
+-----------------------------------------+
| Template (HTML):                        |
|    - Displays product information       |
|    - Includes "Add to Cart" button      |
+-----------------------------------------+
| Styles (CSS):                           |
|    - Defines visual appearance          |
```

Key Observations:

- The ProductCardComponent has private data (product name, description, price, image) that is not directly accessible from other components.
- It has public methods (API) like addToCart() and viewDetails() that allow other parts of the application to interact with it.
- It has a template that defines how the product information is displayed.
- It has styles that define its visual appearance.

Beyond Simple Reusability: Creating Composable UIs

Components don't just live in isolation; they interact and work together to form complex UIs. This is where the concept of **composition** comes in.

What is component composition?

Component composition is the process of combining multiple components to create a larger, more complex component or application. You can think of it as building a LEGO structure by connecting individual LEGO bricks.

Benefits of Component Composition:

- **Code Reuse:** You can reuse existing components to build new features, saving you time and effort.
- **Modularity:** Composition promotes modularity by breaking down the application into smaller, manageable units.
- **Testability:** Composed components are easier to test because you can test each component in isolation.
- **Flexibility:** Composition allows you to easily change the structure and behavior of your application by rearranging components.

An Example of Component Composition:

In our shopping application, we can create a ProductListComponent that displays a list of ProductCardComponent instances. The ProductListComponent would be responsible for fetching the product data and passing it to the ProductCardComponent instances.

```
+------------------------------------+    +----------
-----------------------------+
| ProductListComponent               |    |
ProductCardComponent                |
+------------------------------------+    +---------------
--------------------+
| - Fetches product data             |---->| - Displays
product information          |
| - Creates ProductCardComponent instances|      | - Handles
"Add to Cart" button click|
+------------------------------------+    +---------------
--------------------+
```

Personal Insight: I used to underestimate the power of component composition. But once I started using it, I realized how much easier it made it to build complex UIs. It's a fundamental concept that every Angular developer should understand.

The Component Hierarchy: A Tree of Components

In an Angular application, components are organized into a hierarchy, with the root component at the top and child components branching out from there. This hierarchy forms a tree-like structure.

The Importance of a Well-Defined Hierarchy:

A well-defined component hierarchy makes it easier to understand the structure of your application and how different components interact with each other. It also makes it easier to manage the data flow between components.

In conclusion:

Components are much more than just reusable bits of UI; they are the cornerstone of Angular architecture. By understanding the concepts of encapsulation, reusability, and composition, you can build maintainable, scalable, and testable Angular applications. Embrace the power of components, and you'll unlock the true potential of Angular!

4.2 Generating a New Component: ng generate component- Your Instant Component Factory

We've established how crucial components are in Angular. But let's face it: creating all the necessary files and setting up the basic structure for a component manually can be repetitive and tedious. That's precisely why the Angular CLI provides the ng generate component command (or its shorthand, ng g c). It's your instant component factory, turning a single command into a fully structured component ready for customization.

ng generate component: More Than Just a File Generator

The ng generate component command is not just a convenience; it's a productivity multiplier that enforces consistency across your Angular projects. It handles several tasks for you:

- **Creates the Component Files:** It generates the TypeScript file (.component.ts), the HTML template (.component.html), the CSS stylesheet (.component.css), and the testing file (.component.spec.ts).
- **Registers the Component:** It automatically registers the new component in the appropriate module (usually app.module.ts), making it available for use in your application.
- **Follows Naming Conventions:** It enforces Angular's naming conventions, ensuring that your components are named consistently.
- **Provides a Basic Structure:** It provides a basic component structure with the necessary imports, decorators, and class definitions.

Why is ng generate component a Must-Use Tool?

- **Saves Time and Effort:** It drastically reduces the time and effort required to create new components.
- **Enforces Consistency:** It ensures that all your components are created in a consistent manner, making your code easier to understand and maintain.
- **Reduces Errors:** It reduces the risk of errors by automating the process of creating and registering components.
- **Promotes Best Practices:** It promotes best practices by encouraging you to use components to organize your application.

Step-by-Step Guide: Creating a New Component with ng generate component

1. **Open a Terminal Window:** Open a terminal window in your project directory.
2. **Run the ng generate component Command:** Run the following command to create a new component:

```
ng generate component product-card
```

Shorthand:

```
ng g c product-card
```

Explanation:

- ng generate component (or ng g c): This is the Angular CLI command for generating a new component.
- product-card: This is the name of the component. Choose a descriptive name that reflects the component's purpose. Angular naming conventions recommend using lowercase letters and hyphens to separate words.

The CLI will then generate the component files and register the component in the appropriate module. You'll see messages in the terminal window indicating the files that were created and updated.

3. **Examine the Generated Files:** Open the generated component files in your code editor and examine their contents. You'll see that the CLI has created a basic component structure with the necessary imports, decorators, and class definitions.

Controlling Component Location with --path:

By default, the ng generate component command creates the component files in the src/app directory. However, you can use the --path option to specify a different directory. This is useful for organizing your components into logical groups.

Example:

```
ng g c product-card --path src/app/modules/products
```

This command will create the component files in the src/app/modules/products/product-card directory.

Understanding the Importance of Modules:

Angular organizes code into *modules*. Every component must belong to one, and only one, module. If you don't specify a module to the CLI, it will use the AppModule (your application's root module).

Other Useful Options:

The ng generate component command supports several other options that allow you to customize the component creation process. You can explore these options by running ng generate component --help. Some useful options include:

- --inline-template (-it): Creates the component with an inline template instead of a separate HTML file. This is useful for simple components with small templates.
- --inline-style (-is): Creates the component with inline styles instead of a separate CSS file. This is also useful for simple components with small styles.
- --skip-tests (-st): Skips the creation of the test file. This is useful if you don't want to write tests for your component. However, writing tests is highly recommended!
- --selector: Specifies the CSS selector to use for the component. The default selector is app-component-name.
- --module: Specifies the module to which the component should be added. If not specified, the CLI will try to find the closest module.

Personal Insight: I've seen developers try to avoid using the CLI and create components manually. While it's possible, it's almost always a bad idea. The CLI saves you time, reduces errors, and ensures consistency across your project. Embrace the power of the CLI!

A Note on Naming Conventions:

It's important to follow Angular's naming conventions when creating components. This will make your code easier to understand and maintain.

- Component names should be descriptive and use lowercase letters and hyphens to separate words (e.g., product-card, user-profile).

- Component class names should use PascalCase (e.g., ProductCardComponent, UserProfileComponent).
- Component file names should use lowercase letters and hyphens to separate words (e.g., product-card.component.ts, user-profile.component.html).

Conclusion: Your Component Factory is Ready

The ng generate component command is a powerful tool that simplifies the process of creating new Angular components. By using this command, you can save time, reduce errors, and ensure consistency across your projects. Embrace the power of the CLI and start building amazing Angular applications!

4.3 Component Anatomy: TypeScript, HTML, CSS- The Foundation of Every Angular Component

We've generated our components, and we know they are the building blocks of Angular. But what *actually* makes up a component? Think of every Angular component as having a "soul" (the TypeScript logic), a "face" (the HTML template), and "clothes" (the CSS styles). These three parts, TypeScript, HTML, and CSS, work together to define the component's behavior, appearance, and interactions. Understanding how these three pieces fit together is key to mastering Angular development.

The TypeScript Class: The Brains of the Operation

The TypeScript class (.component.ts file) is the heart of an Angular component. It's where you define the component's logic, data (state), and methods (behavior). It's where you handle user interactions, fetch data from APIs, and perform any other tasks that are required to make the component function. Think of this as the control center.

Key Responsibilities of the TypeScript Class:

- **Defining Data (State):** The TypeScript class defines the data that the component needs to display in the template. This data can include strings, numbers, booleans, arrays, and objects. The class determines what the component *knows*.
- **Handling User Interactions:** The TypeScript class defines the methods that are called when the user interacts with the component.

These methods can handle button clicks, form submissions, and other events. The class determines how the component *reacts*.

- **Fetching Data from APIs:** The TypeScript class can fetch data from backend APIs using Angular's HttpClient service. This allows the component to display dynamic data from external sources. The class is responsible for obtaining any required *information*.
- **Implementing Component Logic:** The TypeScript class implements the logic that determines how the component behaves. This can include calculations, data transformations, and other operations. The class defines the component's *behavior*.
- **Providing the API for the Component:** This class determines how other components interact with this one. Inputs define what data it will receive, and Outputs define how it will send notifications to other components.

Example TypeScript Class:

```
import { Component, OnInit } from '@angular/core';

@Component({
  selector: 'app-product-card',
  templateUrl: './product-card.component.html',
  styleUrls: ['./product-card.component.css']
})
export class ProductCardComponent implements OnInit {

  productName: string = 'Awesome Product';
  productDescription: string = 'This is a description of the
awesome product.';
  productPrice: number = 99.99;
  productImage: string = 'https://via.placeholder.com/150';

  constructor() { }

  ngOnInit(): void {
    // Initialization logic here (e.g., fetching data)
  }

  addToCart(): void {
    // Logic to add the product to the cart
    console.log('Product added to cart!');
  }
}
```

Key Annotations and Interfaces

- **@Component:** The most critical part, this annotation marks the class as an Angular component. It dictates the HTML tag used to represent the component (selector), the HTML to display (templateUrl), and the CSS to style it (styleUrls).
- **OnInit:** This interface allows you to run code when the component is initialized, such as fetching data from an API.

The HTML Template: Defining the View

The HTML template (.component.html file) defines the structure and content of the component's view. It's where you use HTML elements, Angular directives, and data binding expressions to display data from the component and handle user interactions. The template determines what the user *sees*.

Key Elements of the HTML Template:

- **HTML Elements:** You can use standard HTML elements in your template, such as <div>, <h1>, <p>, <img>, and <button>.
- **Angular Directives:** Angular directives are special attributes that extend HTML with new functionality. Directives can be used to conditionally render elements (*ngIf), iterate over data (*ngFor), and modify the behavior of elements.
- **Data Binding Expressions:** Data binding expressions are used to display data from the component in the template and handle user interactions. Angular supports several types of data binding, including:
  - **Interpolation:** Displays data from the component using double curly braces ({{ }}).
  - **Property Binding:** Binds a property of an HTML element to a data value in the component using square brackets ([property]="value").
  - **Event Binding:** Binds an event (e.g., click, mouseover) to a method in the component using parentheses ((event)="handler()").
  - **Two-Way Binding:** Binds a property of an HTML element to a data value in the component and updates the data value when the user interacts with the element using [(ngModel)]="value".

Example HTML Template:

```
<div class="product-card">
```

```
<img [src]="productImage" alt="Product Image">
<h2>{{ productName }}</h2>
<p>{{ productDescription }}</p>
<p>Price: ${{ productPrice }}</p>
<button (click)="addToCart()">Add to Cart</button>
</div>
```

The CSS Stylesheet: Adding Visual Flair

The CSS stylesheet (.component.css file) defines the styling for the component's view. You can define CSS rules here that apply only to the elements in the component's template. This allows you to create encapsulated styles that don't interfere with other components. The CSS determines how the component *looks*.

Key Features of Component Stylesheets:

- **Scoped Styles:** Styles defined in a component's stylesheet are scoped to that component, meaning they don't affect other components in the application. This prevents style conflicts and makes it easier to maintain the styling of your application.
- **CSS Preprocessors:** Angular supports CSS preprocessors such as Sass, SCSS, and Less. These preprocessors allow you to use variables, nesting, mixins, and other features to make your CSS code more organized and maintainable.

Example CSS Stylesheet:

```
.product-card {
  border: 1px solid #ccc;
  padding: 10px;
  margin: 10px;
  text-align: center;
}

.product-card img {
  width: 100%;
  max-height: 150px;
  object-fit: cover;
}
```

The Synergy of TypeScript, HTML, and CSS: A Harmonious Trio

These three parts—TypeScript, HTML, and CSS—work together to create a complete Angular component. The TypeScript class provides the logic and data, the HTML template defines the structure and content of the view, and the CSS stylesheet defines the styling for the view. They communicate like this:

1. The TypeScript class defines the data that needs to be displayed in the template.
2. The template uses data binding expressions to display the data from the TypeScript class.
3. The template uses event binding to call methods in the TypeScript class when the user interacts with the component.
4. The CSS stylesheet defines the styling for the elements in the template.

Personal Insight: I've found that it's helpful to think of components as mini-applications within your application. Each component has its own state, logic, and view, and it's responsible for managing a specific part of the user interface.

Conclusion: The Trinity Unveiled

Understanding the anatomy of an Angular component is essential for building maintainable, scalable, and testable applications. By mastering the TypeScript, HTML, and CSS aspects of components, you'll be well on your way to becoming an Angular expert. This trifecta of code provides the structure, behavior, and style that make Angular applications powerful and engaging.

4.4 Displaying Data with Interpolation: The Simplest Path to Dynamic Content

We've discussed how components are made up of TypeScript, HTML, and CSS. Now, let's explore how these parts talk to each other. Data binding is the mechanism that allows your component's TypeScript code (the logic) to communicate with its HTML template (the view). Interpolation is the simplest and most fundamental form of data binding in Angular. It's your initial tool for injecting dynamic data into your templates and bringing them to life.

What is Interpolation? The Bridge Between Logic and View

Interpolation allows you to display data from your component's TypeScript class in the HTML template using a special syntax: double curly braces {{ }}. Any expression within these curly braces is evaluated by Angular, and its resulting value is then displayed in the template. It's like creating a small window through which your data can shine.

The Power of Simplicity

Interpolation is incredibly straightforward, making it easy to learn and use. It's the perfect starting point for understanding how data binding works in Angular.

How Interpolation Works: A Step-by-Step Explanation

1. **Define a Property in Your Component:** In your component's TypeScript file, define a property that you want to display in the template. This property can be of any data type, including strings, numbers, booleans, arrays, and objects.
2. **Use Interpolation in Your Template:** In your component's HTML template, use interpolation to display the value of the property. Simply enclose the property name within double curly braces {{ }}.
3. **Angular Evaluates the Expression:** When Angular renders the template, it evaluates the expression within the curly braces and replaces it with the actual value of the property.

Example: Displaying Product Information

Let's revisit our ProductCardComponent example. We can use interpolation to display the product's name, description, price, and image in the template.

product-card.component.ts:

```typescript
import { Component } from '@angular/core';

@Component({
  selector: 'app-product-card',
  templateUrl: './product-card.component.html',
  styleUrls: ['./product-card.component.css']
})
export class ProductCardComponent {
  productName: string = 'Awesome Product';
  productDescription: string = 'This is a description of the
awesome product.';
  productPrice: number = 99.99;
```

```
    productImage: string = 'https://via.placeholder.com/150';
}
```

product-card.component.html:

```
    <div class="product-card">
  <img [src]="productImage" alt="Product Image">
  <h2>{{ productName }}</h2>
  <p>{{ productDescription }}</p>
  <p>Price: ${{ productPrice }}</p>
</div>
```

In this example, we're using interpolation to display the productName, productDescription, and productPrice properties in the template. The productImage is using property binding (more on that later), but it's also displaying a value from the component.

Beyond Simple Properties: Using Expressions

Interpolation isn't limited to just displaying simple property values. You can also use expressions within the curly braces to perform calculations, call methods, and access object properties.

Examples of Using Expressions in Interpolation:

- **Performing Calculations:**

```
    <p>Total: ${{ productPrice * quantity }}</p>
```

- **Calling Methods:**

```
    <p>Formatted Price: ${{ formatPrice(productPrice)
}}</p>
```

- **Accessing Object Properties:**

```
    <p>Category: {{ product.category.name }}</p>
```

Important Considerations:

- **Security:** Be careful when displaying data from external sources using interpolation, as it can be vulnerable to cross-site scripting (XSS) attacks. Always sanitize user input before displaying it in the template. Angular's built-in security features help mitigate this, but you should still be aware of the risk.
- **Performance:** Avoid complex expressions in interpolation, as they can impact performance. If you need to perform complex calculations, it's best to do them in the TypeScript class and then display the result in the template.

Personal Insight: I remember when I first started using Angular, I relied heavily on interpolation. It was so easy to display data in the template! However, as my applications grew more complex, I learned to use other data binding techniques to improve performance and maintainability.

Alternative to Interpolation: Property Binding

While interpolation is great for displaying text content, it's not always the best choice for setting element properties. For example, to set the src attribute of an <img> tag, it's better to use property binding:

```
<img [src]="productImage" alt="Product Image">
```

We'll cover property binding in more detail in the next chapter.

Conclusion: Your Gateway to Dynamic Content

Interpolation is a powerful tool for displaying dynamic data in your Angular templates. It's the simplest and most fundamental form of data binding, and it's an essential skill for every Angular developer. By mastering interpolation, you can bring your data to life and create engaging user interfaces. But keep in mind that interpolation is just the starting point! There's a whole universe of data binding techniques to explore, which you'll discover in the chapters that follow.

Chapter 5: Mastering Data Binding - Forging the Dynamic Connection

We've already dipped our toes into data binding with interpolation. Now, it's time to fully immerse ourselves in the world of Angular data binding! This chapter will delve into the various techniques that allow you to seamlessly connect your component's logic (TypeScript) with its view (HTML). Data binding is what transforms static HTML into dynamic, interactive user interfaces.

Why Data Binding is Essential

Data binding is the engine that drives the dynamic behavior of Angular applications. It enables you to:

- **Display data from your component in the template.**
- **Update data in the component when the user interacts with the template.**
- **Create responsive and interactive user interfaces.**
- **Simplify your code and reduce the amount of manual DOM manipulation.**

The Four Pillars of Angular Data Binding:

Angular offers four main types of data binding, each serving a specific purpose:

1. **Interpolation:** Displaying values in the template (we've already covered this).
2. **Property Binding:** Setting element properties to component values.
3. **Event Binding:** Responding to user actions in the template.
4. **Two-Way Binding:** Synchronizing data between the component and the template (typically used with form inputs).

5.1 Interpolation: Displaying Values- Your First Brushstroke on the Angular Canvas

While we touched upon interpolation previously, it's worth revisiting this fundamental concept. Think of interpolation as your first brushstroke when painting a dynamic user interface with Angular. It's the simplest, most direct way to inject data from your component's TypeScript logic into the HTML template, bringing your view to life with dynamic content.

Beyond the Basics: Why Interpolation Matters

Interpolation is more than just a way to display data. It embodies the core principle of data binding, which is the automatic synchronization between your component's data and its view. This means that when your component's data changes, the view is automatically updated, and vice versa.

The Mechanics of Interpolation: How it Works Behind the Scenes

At its heart, interpolation uses Angular's expression evaluation engine. When Angular encounters the double curly braces {{ }} in your template, it treats everything inside as a JavaScript-like expression.

Angular then:

1. **Evaluates the expression:** Angular evaluates the expression within the curly braces. This can involve accessing properties of the component class, calling methods, or performing calculations.
2. **Converts the result to a string:** The result of the expression is converted to a string using the toString() method.
3. **Replaces the expression with the string value:** The entire {{ expression }} is replaced with the resulting string in the DOM (Document Object Model).

Example: Displaying a Welcome Message

```typescript
// my-component.component.ts
import { Component } from '@angular/core';

@Component({
  selector: 'app-my-component',
  templateUrl: './my-component.component.html',
  styleUrls: ['./my-component.component.css']
})
export class MyComponent {
  userName: string = 'John Doe';
}
```

```html
<!-- my-component.component.html -->
<h1>Welcome, {{ userName }}!</h1>
```

In this example, Angular will evaluate the expression userName, which is a property of the MyComponent class. It will then convert the value of the userName property (which is "John Doe") to a string and replace {{ userName }} with "John Doe" in the DOM. The resulting HTML will be:

```
<h1>Welcome, John Doe!</h1>
```

More Than Just Property Names: Using Expressions

Interpolation isn't limited to displaying simple property names. You can also use more complex expressions within the curly braces to perform calculations, call methods, and access object properties.

Examples of Advanced Interpolation:

- **Performing Calculations:**

```
<p>Total Price: ${{ productPrice + (productPrice * taxRate) }}</p>
```

- **Calling Methods:**

```
<p>Formatted Date: {{ formatDate(myDate) }}</p>
```

- **Accessing Object Properties:**

```
<p>Category: {{ product.category.name }}</p>
```

Best Practices for Using Interpolation:

- **Keep Expressions Simple:** Avoid complex expressions in interpolation, as they can impact performance. If you need to perform complex calculations, it's best to do them in the TypeScript class and then display the result in the template.

- **Use Safe Navigation Operator:** When accessing properties of objects that might be null or undefined, use the safe navigation operator (?.) to prevent errors.

```
<p>Category: {{ product?.category?.name }}</p>
```

The safe navigation operator will prevent an error if product or product.category is null or undefined.

- **Sanitize User Input:** Be careful when displaying data from external sources using interpolation, as it can be vulnerable to cross-site scripting (XSS) attacks. Always sanitize user input before displaying it in the template. Angular provides built-in security features to help mitigate XSS attacks.

When to Use Interpolation vs. Property Binding

Interpolation is best suited for displaying text content. However, for setting element properties (e.g., src attribute of an <img> tag, disabled attribute of a <button> tag), it's generally better to use property binding. We'll explore property binding in the next section.

Personal Insight: I often use interpolation for displaying simple data values, such as titles, descriptions, and prices. However, for more complex scenarios, I prefer to use property binding or other data binding techniques.

A Note on Alternatives

While interpolation is a common way to display values, there are other ways as well, including:

- **Property Binding:** Displaying values by assigning them to HTML element properties
- **Pipes:** Transforming the data before rendering it to the template (e.g., formatting dates or currency)

Conclusion: A Powerful Tool for Dynamic Content

Interpolation is a fundamental concept in Angular that allows you to dynamically display data from your component in the template. It's simple, powerful, and essential for creating engaging user interfaces. While it has its limitations, mastering interpolation is a crucial first step in your Angular journey. Now, let's move on to property binding and explore another powerful data binding technique!

5.2 Property Binding: Setting Element Properties- Shaping the DOM Dynamically

While interpolation is a great way to inject text into your HTML, it's not always the best tool for controlling the *behavior* and *appearance* of your elements. This is where property binding comes in. Property binding allows you to dynamically set the properties of HTML elements based on values in your component, giving you fine-grained control over the DOM.

Beyond Static HTML: Bringing Elements to Life

In traditional HTML, elements are defined statically. Their attributes are set once and remain unchanged. Property binding lets you break free from this static nature and create elements that respond to changes in your application's data and logic.

The Mechanics of Property Binding: Bridging the Gap Between Data and Elements

Property binding establishes a one-way connection from your component's TypeScript class to the properties of HTML elements. When the value of a property in your component changes, the corresponding property of the HTML element is automatically updated.

The Syntax: Square Brackets are Key

Property binding uses square brackets [] around the HTML attribute you want to bind.

```
<element
[attribute]="componentPropertyExpression"></element>
```

Key Components:

- **element:** The HTML element you want to modify (e.g., <img>, <button>, <div>).

- **attribute:** The HTML attribute you want to bind to (e.g., src, disabled, class).
- **componentPropertyExpression:** A TypeScript expression that evaluates to the value you want to assign to the element property. This can be a simple property name, a more complex expression, or a method call.

Common Use Cases for Property Binding:

Property binding is a versatile tool that can be used in a variety of scenarios. Here are some common use cases:

- **Setting the src Attribute of an <img> Tag:** This allows you to dynamically change the image displayed in your application.

```
<img [src]="imageUrl" alt="Product Image">
```

- **Enabling or Disabling a <button> Tag:** This allows you to control whether the user can interact with the button based on the state of your application.

```
<button [disabled]="isButtonDisabled">Click Me</button>
```

- **Dynamically Adding CSS Classes:** This allows you to apply different styles to an element based on the state of your application.

```
<div [class.highlighted]="isHighlighted">Content</div>
```

  In this example, the highlighted class will be added to the <div> element if the isHighlighted property in your component is true.

- **Setting ARIA Attributes for Accessibility:** This allows you to make your application more accessible to users with disabilities.

```
<button [attr.aria-label]="buttonLabel">Click</button>
```

- **Setting the value attribute of an <input> or <textarea> tag:** While two-way binding ([(ngModel)]) is the most common way to manage form inputs, property binding can be useful when you only need to display a value and don't want the user to be able to edit it directly.

Property vs. Attribute Binding: Understanding the Nuances

It's important to understand the difference between properties and attributes in HTML.

- **Attributes:** Attributes are defined in the HTML markup and are used to initialize the element. Attributes are often string values.
- **Properties:** Properties are part of the DOM (Document Object Model) and represent the current state of the element. Properties can be of any data type (string, number, boolean, object, etc.).

Think of attributes as initial settings, and properties as the element's current state.

Key Differences to Keep in Mind:

- Property binding affects the element's *property* in the DOM.
- Attribute binding (using attr.) affects the element's *attribute* in the HTML markup.

Example: Setting the colspan Attribute of a <td> Tag

In most cases, you'll want to use property binding. However, there are some cases where you might need to use attribute binding. For example, the colspan attribute of a <td> tag doesn't have a corresponding property in the DOM. In this case, you would use attribute binding:

```
<td [attr.colspan]="columnCount">Content</td>
```

Personal Insight: I remember being confused about the difference between properties and attributes when I first started learning Angular. It took me some time to understand the nuances, but once I did, it made a big difference in my ability to control the behavior of my elements.

A Word on Security:

Property binding, like interpolation, can be vulnerable to cross-site scripting (XSS) attacks if you're not careful. Always sanitize user input before displaying it in the template. Angular provides built-in security features to help mitigate XSS attacks, but you should still be aware of the risk.

Conclusion: Master of the DOM

Property binding is a powerful tool that gives you dynamic control over the properties of HTML elements. By mastering property binding, you can create responsive, interactive, and accessible user interfaces that bring your Angular applications to life. It's a step up from simple text injection, letting you actually control how elements behave.

5.3 Event Binding: Responding to User Actions- Building Truly Interactive Experiences

Interpolation and property binding allow you to control what the user *sees*. Event binding, however, lets you react to what the user *does*. Event binding allows your components to listen for and respond to user actions in the template, such as button clicks, form submissions, and mouse movements. This ability to react is what transforms a passive display of data into a truly interactive and engaging user experience.

Beyond Presentation: Enabling Interaction

Event binding is the key to creating dynamic applications that respond to user input. Without event binding, your application would be a static display of data. With event binding, you can:

- **Handle user clicks:** Trigger actions when the user clicks on a button or link.
- **Process form submissions:** Collect data from forms and send it to a server.
- **React to mouse movements:** Create interactive effects based on the position of the mouse cursor.
- **Respond to keyboard input:** Capture keystrokes and perform actions accordingly.

The Mechanics of Event Binding: Listening for User Input

Event binding establishes a connection from an HTML element's event to a method in your component's TypeScript class. When the specified event occurs on the element, the corresponding method is automatically executed.

This allows you to handle user actions and update your application's state accordingly.

The Syntax: Parentheses are Your Friends

Event binding uses parentheses () around the event you want to listen for.

```
<element
(event)="componentMethod(arguments)"></element>
```

Key Components:

- **element:** The HTML element you want to listen for events on (e.g., <button>, <a>, <input>).
- **event:** The name of the HTML event you want to listen for (e.g., click, mouseover, keydown, submit).
- **componentMethod:** The name of the method in your component's TypeScript class that you want to execute when the event occurs.
- **arguments (Optional):** Any arguments you want to pass to the component method.

Common Events to Bind To:

HTML provides a wide range of events that you can bind to. Here are some of the most common:

- **Mouse Events:**
  - click: When the user clicks on the element.
  - mouseover: When the mouse cursor hovers over the element.
  - mouseout: When the mouse cursor leaves the element.
  - mousedown: When the user presses a mouse button while the cursor is over the element.
  - mouseup: When the user releases a mouse button while the cursor is over the element.
- **Keyboard Events:**
  - keydown: When the user presses a key while the element has focus.
  - keyup: When the user releases a key while the element has focus.
  - keypress: When the user presses and releases a key that produces a character.

- **Form Events:**
  - o submit: When the user submits a form.
  - o change: When the value of an input element changes.
  - o input: When the value of an input element is changed.
  - o focus: When an element gains focus.
  - o blur: When an element loses focus.
- **Touch Events (for mobile devices):**
  - o touchstart: When the user touches the element.
  - o touchmove: When the user moves their finger across the element.
  - o touchend: When the user lifts their finger from the element.

Example: Handling a Button Click to Toggle Visibility

```
// my-component.component.ts
import { Component } from '@angular/core';

@Component({
  selector: 'app-my-component',
  templateUrl: './my-component.component.html',
  styleUrls: ['./my-component.component.css']
})
export class MyComponent {
  isVisible: boolean = false;

  toggleVisibility(): void {
    this.isVisible = !this.isVisible;
  }
}


<!-- my-component.component.html -->
<button (click)="toggleVisibility()">Toggle
Visibility</button>
<div *ngIf="isVisible">
  This content is now visible!
</div>
```

In this example, the toggleVisibility() method in the MyComponent class is called when the user clicks on the <button> element. The toggleVisibility() method toggles the value of the isVisible property, which in turn controls whether the <div> element is displayed using the *ngIf directive.

Accessing Event Data: The $event Object - Getting Details About the Interaction

When you bind to an event, Angular automatically passes an event object to the bound method. This event object contains information about the event, such as the target element, the mouse coordinates, the key that was pressed, and other relevant details. You can access the event object using the $event variable.

Example: Getting the Input Value on Keyup

```typescript
// my-component.component.ts
import { Component } from '@angular/core';

@Component({
  selector: 'app-my-component',
  templateUrl: './my-component.component.html',
  styleUrls: ['./my-component.component.css']
})
export class MyComponent {
  inputValue: string = '';

  updateInputValue(event: any): void {
    this.inputValue = (<HTMLInputElement>event.target).value;
  }
}
```

```html
<!-- my-component.component.html -->
<input type="text" (keyup)="updateInputValue($event)">
<p>Input Value: {{ inputValue }}</p>
```

In this example, the updateInputValue() method is called whenever the user releases a key in the <input> element. The event object is passed to the updateInputValue() method, and the value of the input element is accessed using event.target.value. Note the cast to HTMLInputElement for type safety.

Personal Insight: Event binding is what truly brought my web applications to life. It's empowering to be able to respond to user interactions and create dynamic, engaging experiences.

A Word on Performance

While event binding is powerful, it's important to be mindful of performance. Avoid binding to events that fire frequently (e.g., mousemove, scroll) if you don't need to. Also, avoid performing complex operations in your event handlers, as this can slow down your application.

Conclusion: Building a Two-Way Dialogue

Event binding is a fundamental concept in Angular that allows you to create reactive interfaces that respond to user actions. By mastering event binding, you can build truly interactive and engaging web applications. It moves your application from a one-way display to a two-way conversation with the user.

5.4 Two-Way Binding: [(ngModel)] for Input Fields- The Magic of Synchronization

We've explored how property binding allows you to push data *from* your component to the view, and event binding allows you to react to events *from* the view. Two-way binding takes this a step further, creating a *synchronization* between the component and the view. When the user changes the value of an input field, the corresponding property in your component is automatically updated, and vice versa.

Beyond One-Way Communication: A Two-Way Street

Two-way binding greatly simplifies the process of working with form inputs. Instead of manually listening for change events and updating the component's data, you can simply use the [(ngModel)] directive, and Angular will handle the synchronization for you. This reduces boilerplate code and makes your applications easier to read and maintain.

The Mechanics of Two-Way Binding: A Symphony of Data Flow

Two-way binding with [(ngModel)] is essentially shorthand for combining property binding and event binding.

What [(ngModel)] actually does under the hood:

1. **Property Binding:** It sets the value property of the input element to the value of the component's property.
2. **Event Binding:** It listens for the input event on the input element and updates the component's property whenever the user changes the value of the input field.

The Syntax: Square Brackets and Parentheses Together

Two-way binding uses a special syntax that combines property binding and event binding: [(ngModel)]. It looks like a "banana in a box":

```
<input type="text" [(ngModel)]="componentProperty">
```

Key Components:

- **input (or other form element):** The HTML input element you want to bind to (e.g., <input type="text">, <textarea>, <select>).
- [(ngModel)]: The two-way binding directive.
- componentProperty: The name of the property in your component's TypeScript class that you want to bind to.

Important: Importing FormsModule

Before you can use [(ngModel)], you need to import the FormsModule in your application module (app.module.ts). This is a common pitfall for beginners!

```
import { BrowserModule } from '@angular/platform-
browser';
import { NgModule } from '@angular/core';
import { FormsModule } from '@angular/forms'; // Import
FormsModule

import { AppComponent } from './app.component';

@NgModule({
  declarations: [
    AppComponent
  ],
  imports: [
    BrowserModule,
    FormsModule // Add FormsModule to imports
  ],
  providers: [],
  bootstrap: [AppComponent]
})
export class AppModule { }
```

Example: Creating a Two-Way Bound Input Field

```
// my-component.component.ts
import { Component } from '@angular/core';
```

```
@Component({
  selector: 'app-my-component',
  templateUrl: './my-component.component.html',
  styleUrls: ['./my-component.component.css']
})
export class MyComponent {
  name: string = '';
}


        <!-- my-component.component.html -->
<input type="text" [(ngModel)]="name">
<p>Name: {{ name }}</p>
```

In this example, the value of the <input> element is bound to the name property in the MyComponent class. When the user types in the input field, the name property is automatically updated, and the updated value is displayed in the <p> tag using interpolation.

Why Use [(ngModel)]?

- **Simplified Code:** It significantly reduces the amount of code you need to write to work with form inputs.
- **Automatic Synchronization:** It automatically synchronizes data between the component and the view, eliminating the need for manual updates.
- **Improved Readability:** It makes your code easier to read and understand by clearly indicating the two-way binding relationship.
- **Easy Integration with Forms:** It integrates seamlessly with Angular's form features, such as validation and submission.

Common Use Cases for [(ngModel)]:

- **Text Input Fields:** Capturing user input in text fields.
- **Textareas:** Handling multi-line text input.
- **Select Boxes:** Capturing user selections from dropdown menus.
- **Checkboxes:** Capturing boolean values from checkboxes.
- **Radio Buttons:** Capturing selections from radio button groups.

Beyond Simple Data Types: Working with Objects

[(ngModel)] can also be used with complex data types, such as objects. In this case, you would bind to a property of the object.

83

Example: Binding to an Object Property

```typescript
    // my-component.component.ts
import { Component } from '@angular/core';

@Component({
  selector: 'app-my-component',
  templateUrl: './my-component.component.html',
  styleUrls: ['./my-component.component.css']
})
export class MyComponent {
  user = {
    firstName: '',
    lastName: ''
  };
}
```

```html
    <!-- my-component.component.html -->
<label>First Name:</label>
<input type="text" [(ngModel)]="user.firstName">

<label>Last Name:</label>
<input type="text" [(ngModel)]="user.lastName">

<p>Full Name: {{ user.firstName }} {{ user.lastName }}</p>
```

In this example, the <input> elements are bound to the firstName and lastName properties of the user object. When the user types in the input fields, the corresponding properties of the user object are automatically updated.

Personal Insight: [(ngModel)] is one of my favorite Angular features. It makes working with forms so much easier and more efficient. I can't imagine building a web application without it.

A Word of Caution: Performance and Scalability

While [(ngModel)] is convenient, it's important to use it judiciously. In very large and complex forms, two-way binding can impact performance. In these cases, consider using one-way binding with explicit event handling.

Conclusion: Seamless Data Synchronization

[(ngModel)] is a powerful directive that simplifies the process of working with form inputs in Angular. By mastering two-way binding, you can create dynamic and interactive forms with ease, providing a seamless user experience. However, be mindful of its potential impact on performance and use it judiciously. You now have the power to effortlessly connect user input to your application's data!

5.5 Building a Simple Counter: A Data Binding Symphony in Action

Now that we've explored the individual data binding techniques, let's combine them all in a practical example: building a simple counter component. This exercise will solidify your understanding of interpolation, property binding, event binding, and two-way binding, showcasing how they work together to create a dynamic and interactive user interface. Think of this as conducting a symphony where each instrument (data binding technique) plays its part to create a harmonious whole.

From Theory to Practice: A Hands-On Approach

Building a counter component is a classic programming exercise, but it's particularly well-suited for demonstrating data binding in Angular. It's a simple yet powerful example that highlights the key concepts we've covered in this chapter.

The Requirements:

Our counter component will have the following features:

- A display to show the current count.
- Increment and decrement buttons to increase or decrease the count.
- An input field to specify the amount by which the counter should be incremented or decremented.

Step-by-Step Implementation:

1. **Create a New Component:** Use the Angular CLI to create a new component named counter:

   ```
   ng generate component counter
   ```

2. **Define the Component's Properties:** In the counter.component.ts file, define the following properties:

```
import { Component } from '@angular/core';

@Component({
  selector: 'app-counter',
  templateUrl: './counter.component.html',
  styleUrls: ['./counter.component.css']
})
export class CounterComponent {
  count: number = 0; // The current count
  incrementAmount: number = 1; // The amount to
increment/decrement
}
```

We have two key data points: the current count (initialized to 0) and the incrementAmount (initialized to 1).

3. **Implement the Increment and Decrement Methods:** Add the increment() and decrement() methods to the CounterComponent class:

```
import { Component } from '@angular/core';

@Component({
  selector: 'app-counter',
  templateUrl: './counter.component.html',
  styleUrls: ['./counter.component.css']
})
export class CounterComponent {
  count: number = 0;
  incrementAmount: number = 1;

  increment(): void {
    this.count += this.incrementAmount;
  }

  decrement(): void {
    this.count -= this.incrementAmount;
  }
}
```

These methods update the count property by adding or subtracting the incrementAmount.

4. **Create the HTML Template:** In the counter.component.html file, create the HTML template for the component:

```html
<div class="counter-container">
<button (click)="decrement()">-</button>
<span>{{ count }}</span>
<button (click)="increment()">+</button>

<div>
  Increment Amount:
  <input type="number" [(ngModel)]="incrementAmount">
</div>
</div>
```

Let's break down the template:

- `<button (click)="decrement()">-</button>`: This button uses event binding to call the decrement() method when clicked.
- `<span>{{ count }}</span>`: This `<span>` element uses interpolation to display the current value of the count property.
- `<button (click)="increment()">+</button>`: This button uses event binding to call the increment() method when clicked.
- `<input type="number" [(ngModel)]="incrementAmount">`: This input element uses two-way binding to bind its value to the incrementAmount property.

5. **Add Some Styling (Optional):** In the counter.component.css file, add some styling to make the component look nice:

```css
.counter-container {
display: flex;
align-items: center;
justify-content: center;
margin: 20px;
}

.counter-container button {
  font-size: 20px;
  padding: 10px 20px;
  margin: 0 10px;
  cursor: pointer;
}

.counter-container span {
  font-size: 24px;
  margin: 0 20px;
```

```
}

.counter-container input {
  width: 80px;
  padding: 5px;
  font-size: 16px;
  text-align: center;
}
```

6. **Use the Component in Your Application:** In your app.component.html file, add the <app-counter> tag to display the counter component:

```
   <div style="text-align:center">
<h1>
  Welcome to {{ title }}!
</h1>
<app-counter></app-counter>
</div>
```

Important: Remember to declare your counter component in app.module.ts.

Putting it all together

You've now successfully created a simple counter component that demonstrates the power of data binding in Angular! You can click the "+" and "-" buttons to increment and decrement the count, and you can enter a value in the input field to change the amount by which the counter is incremented or decremented.

Analysis: Deconstructing the Counter Component

- **Interpolation:** The {{ count }} expression in the template displays the current value of the count property. When the count property is updated, the view is automatically updated.
- **Event Binding:** The (click) event bindings on the buttons call the increment() and decrement() methods when the buttons are clicked.
- **Two-Way Binding:** The [(ngModel)] directive on the input element binds the value of the input field to the incrementAmount property. When the user changes the value in the input field, the incrementAmount property is automatically updated, and vice versa.

Personal Insight: Building this simple counter component was one of the first things I did when I started learning Angular. It helped me solidify my understanding of data binding and see how the different techniques work together.

Beyond the Basics: Enhancing the Counter Component

Here are some ideas for enhancing the counter component:

- Add validation to the input field to ensure that the user enters a valid number.
- Add a reset button to reset the count to zero.
- Add a history display to show the previous values of the count.
- Use property binding to dynamically style the counter based on its value (e.g., change the color of the count if it's negative).

Conclusion: Orchestrating Data Binding Techniques

Building the simple counter component has demonstrated how you can combine interpolation, property binding, event binding, and two-way binding to create dynamic and interactive user interfaces in Angular. It shows how data binding transforms static markup into a responsive, user-driven experience. You now have the tools to create powerful and engaging applications that truly respond to user actions. Data binding is your instrument; now, go make some music!

Chapter 6: Directives: Adding Logic to Templates - Empowering Your HTML

We've covered components, the foundational building blocks of Angular. But what if you need to manipulate the DOM (Document Object Model) directly within your templates, adding conditional logic or dynamically changing the appearance of elements? This is where **directives** come in. Think of directives as instructions that extend the power of HTML, telling it how to behave and display data in more sophisticated ways.

What Are Directives? Giving HTML Instructions

Directives are markers on a DOM element that instruct Angular to modify that element's behavior or appearance. They provide a way to add logic to your templates without having to write complex JavaScript code. Directives add power and flexibility to your HTML.

Key Characteristics of Directives:

- **DOM Manipulation:** Directives can manipulate the DOM by adding, removing, or modifying elements.
- **Behavior Modification:** Directives can modify the behavior of elements by listening for events and updating properties.
- **Reusability:** Directives can be reused throughout your application, promoting code reuse and consistency.
- **Extensibility:** Angular provides a way to create custom directives, allowing you to extend the functionality of HTML with your own custom logic.

Types of Directives:

Angular provides three types of directives:

1. **Component Directives:** These are directives with a template. In fact, components *are* directives with templates. They are the most common type of directive. We've covered these in detail already!
2. **Structural Directives:** These directives change the DOM layout by adding, removing, or replacing elements. Examples include *ngIf and *ngFor. They always have an asterisk (*) prefix.

3. **Attribute Directives:** These directives change the appearance or behavior of an element by modifying its attributes or properties. Examples include [ngClass] and [ngStyle]. They are enclosed in square brackets ([]).

In this chapter, we'll focus on structural and attribute directives.

6.1 What are Directives? Giving HTML Superpowers

We've conquered components, the foundational building blocks of your Angular applications. Now, it's time to explore a different kind of building block – directives. Think of directives not as standalone structures like components, but rather as powerful add-ons that enhance and modify the behavior and appearance of existing HTML elements. They're essentially "superpowers" you can grant to your HTML.

Beyond Basic HTML: Adding Programmable Instructions

HTML is a powerful language for structuring content, but it's inherently static. It lacks the ability to dynamically adapt to changing data or user interactions. This is where directives come to the rescue. Directives let you inject programmatic logic into your templates, enabling you to create dynamic and responsive user interfaces that go far beyond what's possible with standard HTML.

What Do Directives Actually Do?

At their core, directives are markers on a DOM element that instruct Angular to do something with that element. This "something" can range from simply adding a CSS class to completely restructuring the DOM. In a sense, they act as modifiers that influence the nature of the elements they adorn.

Key Responsibilities of Directives:

- **Transforming the DOM:** Directives can add, remove, or modify elements in the DOM, allowing you to create dynamic layouts that respond to changing data.
- **Manipulating Element Attributes:** Directives can modify the attributes of elements, such as the class, style, src, and disabled attributes.

- **Listening to Events:** Directives can listen for events on elements, such as clicks, mouseovers, and keypresses, and execute custom logic in response.
- **Extending HTML Syntax:** Directives allow you to extend the functionality of HTML with your own custom logic, creating new and reusable UI patterns.
- **Promoting Reusability:** They encapsulate specific logic and styles, allowing you to reuse this functionality across multiple parts of your application, fostering a DRY (Don't Repeat Yourself) codebase.

The Three Flavors of Directives: Understanding the Types

Angular provides three distinct types of directives, each with its own purpose and syntax:

1. **Component Directives:** As you already know, components *are* directives with a template. They're the most common type of directive and are used to create reusable UI elements with their own encapsulated logic and view. They're full-fledged parts of your application, having their own HTML, CSS, and TypeScript files.
2. **Structural Directives:** These directives shape or reshape the DOM's *structure*. They add, remove, or replace elements in the DOM. Key examples include *ngIf and *ngFor. They *always* use an asterisk (*) prefix, which is a shorthand for a more complex template syntax.
3. **Attribute Directives:** These directives modify the behavior or appearance of an element by changing its attributes or properties. They don't directly add or remove elements, but they can significantly alter how an element looks and behaves. Examples include [ngClass] and [ngStyle]. They are *always* enclosed in square brackets ([]).

Analogy: The Construction Crew

Think of building a house. Components are like the pre-fabricated walls, windows, and doors that you assemble to create the structure. Directives are like the tools and instructions that the construction crew uses to modify those pre-fabricated parts.

- **Component Directives (Walls, Windows, Doors):** Pre-built structures with their own specific purpose and appearance.

- **Structural Directives (The Demolition Crew, The Addition Builders):** Tools that add or remove structural elements (walls, rooms) to change the layout of the house.
- **Attribute Directives (Painters, Electricians, Plumbers):** Tools that modify the appearance or behavior of existing elements (painting the walls, adding electrical wiring, installing plumbing).

Why are Directives Important?

- **Enhanced HTML:** Directives enable you to extend the capabilities of HTML with your own custom logic and functionality.
- **Code Reusability:** Directives can be reused throughout your application, promoting code reuse and consistency.
- **Maintainability:** Directives make your code easier to maintain by encapsulating specific logic and styling.
- **Testability:** Directives are easier to test because they are self-contained and have well-defined interfaces.

Personal Insight: Directives were a revelation when I first started using Angular. They allowed me to create much more dynamic and interactive user interfaces with less code and more control. They empowered me to go beyond basic HTML and create truly engaging experiences.

A Quick Preview of What's to Come:

In the following sections, we'll dive deeper into structural and attribute directives, exploring how to use them to create dynamic and responsive user interfaces. You'll learn how to:

- Conditionally display elements using *ngIf.
- Iterate over data and display it in a list or table using *ngFor.
- Dynamically add CSS classes using [ngClass].
- Dynamically set inline styles using [ngStyle].

Conclusion: Unleashing the Power Within HTML

Directives are a fundamental part of Angular that allow you to add logic to your templates, manipulate the DOM, and extend the functionality of HTML. By mastering directives, you can unlock the true potential of Angular and create truly dynamic and engaging web applications. This is

6.2 *ngIf: Conditional Rendering- Controlling Visibility with Precision

We've learned about the power of directives, and now we're diving into one of the most fundamental structural directives: *ngIf. Think of *ngIf as your gatekeeper, controlling which elements are allowed to enter (or remain) in the DOM based on a specific condition. This directive gives you precise control over what the user sees, creating dynamic and context-aware user interfaces.

Beyond Simple Visibility: Strategic DOM Management

*ngIf is more than just a simple "show/hide" switch. It's a powerful tool for managing the DOM, allowing you to add or remove elements based on the current state of your application. This has important implications for performance, accessibility, and overall application behavior.

The Mechanics of *ngIf: A Conditional Gatekeeper

*ngIf works by evaluating a boolean expression. If the expression evaluates to true, the element to which the directive is applied is added to the DOM. If the expression evaluates to false, the element is removed from the DOM. This is a crucial distinction: the element isn't just hidden; it's completely removed from the DOM, freeing up resources and preventing the browser from rendering unnecessary content.

The Syntax: The Asterisk is Key

The *ngIf directive always starts with an asterisk (*), followed by the directive name and the expression you want to evaluate:

```
<element *ngIf="expression">Content</element>
```

Key Components:

- *ngIf: The conditional rendering directive.
- expression: A TypeScript expression that evaluates to a boolean value (true or false).
- element: The HTML element you want to conditionally render.

- Content: The HTML content that will be displayed if the expression is true.

Common Use Cases for *ngIf:

*ngIf is a versatile directive that can be used in a variety of scenarios. Here are some common use cases:

- **Displaying Content Based on User Authentication:** Show different content to logged-in users versus guests.

```
<div *ngIf="isLoggedIn">Welcome, User!</div>
<div *ngIf="!isLoggedIn">Please log in.</div>
```

- **Displaying Error Messages:** Show an error message only if there is an error.

```
<div *ngIf="errorMessage">Error: {{ errorMessage }}</div>
```

- **Loading Indicators:** Show a loading indicator while data is being fetched from a server.

```
<div *ngIf="isLoading">Loading...</div>
<div *ngIf="!isLoading">Data: {{ data }}</div>
```

- **Empty State Messages:** Display a message when a list is empty.

```
<div *ngIf="items.length === 0">No items found.</div>
<ul *ngIf="items.length > 0">
  <li *ngFor="let item of items">{{ item }}</li>
</ul>
```

The else Block: Providing an Alternative View

Angular also provides an else block that allows you to specify an alternative view to display when the *ngIf expression evaluates to false. This eliminates the need for a separate *ngIf directive with the negated expression.

Syntax:

95

```
    <div *ngIf="expression; else elseBlock">Content</div>
<ng-template #elseBlock>Alternative Content</ng-template>
```

Example: Using the else Block

```
    <div *ngIf="isLoggedIn; else loginPrompt">
  Welcome, User!
</div>

<ng-template #loginPrompt>
  Please log in.
</ng-template>
```

In this example, if isLoggedIn is true, the "Welcome, User!" message is displayed. Otherwise, the content within the <ng-template #loginPrompt> element is displayed.

Understanding the <ng-template> Element:

The <ng-template> element is a special Angular element that is used to define a template that is not rendered directly. It's often used in conjunction with structural directives like *ngIf and *ngFor.

The then Block: Less Common, But Still Useful

You can also use a then block with *ngIf to specify a template to display when the expression is true.

Syntax:

```
    <div *ngIf="expression; then thenBlock else
elseBlock"></div>
<ng-template #thenBlock>Content</ng-template>
<ng-template #elseBlock>Alternative Content</ng-template>
```

This provides a way to explicitly define both the then and else templates, even if you only need one of them.

Important Considerations:

- **Performance:** While *ngIf can improve performance by removing unnecessary elements from the DOM, it's important to use it judiciously. Avoid using *ngIf to conditionally render very small elements, as the overhead of adding and removing the element from the DOM can outweigh the performance benefits.

- **Accessibility:** Make sure that your application is accessible to users with disabilities. Use ARIA attributes to provide context and information about the content that is being conditionally rendered.

The *ngIf Trap: Avoid Common Mistakes

- **Negating the Condition Twice:** Avoid using separate *ngIf directives to display content based on both true and false conditions. Use the else block instead.

  Bad:

  ```
  <div *ngIf="isLoggedIn">Welcome!</div>
  <div *ngIf="!isLoggedIn">Please Log in!</div>
  ```

  Good:

  ```
  <div *ngIf="isLoggedIn; else
  notLoggedIn">Welcome!</div>
  <ng-template #notLoggedIn>Please Log in!</ng-template>
  ```

- **Overuse:** Don't use *ngIf when CSS can solve the problem. If all you're doing is showing/hiding based on a boolean, CSS may be a better solution.

Personal Insight: I've seen developers overuse *ngIf in situations where CSS could have been used instead. It's important to choose the right tool for the job. CSS is often more performant for simple show/hide scenarios.

Conclusion: Mastering Conditional Rendering

*ngIf is a powerful tool for controlling the visibility of elements in your Angular applications. By mastering *ngIf and its related features (the else and then blocks), you can create dynamic and context-aware user interfaces that adapt to the changing state of your application. You're now in control of what the user sees, when they see it. This allows for a much richer and more targeted experience.

6.3 *ngFor: Looping Through Data - The Key to Dynamic Collections

While *ngIf is your gatekeeper, controlling *whether* content is displayed, *ngFor is your workforce, generating repetitive content based on the data you provide. Think of *ngFor as your cloning machine, creating multiple instances of an element for each item in a collection. This directive is essential for creating dynamic lists, tables, and other data-driven interfaces.

Beyond Static Markup: Displaying Dynamic Data Collections

In traditional HTML, you would need to manually create each element in a list or table. This is tedious and error-prone, especially when dealing with large or dynamic datasets. *ngFor automates this process, allowing you to display collections of data with ease.

The Mechanics of *ngFor: Iterating and Rendering

*ngFor works by iterating over an array or iterable of data. For each item in the array, it creates a new instance of the element to which the directive is applied. The element's content can then be populated with data from the current item in the array.

The Syntax: let is Your Friend

The *ngFor directive uses the let keyword to declare a local variable that represents the current item in the array:

```
    <element *ngFor="let item of items">
  {{ item }}
</element>
```

Key Components:

- *ngFor: The iteration directive.
- let item: Declares a local variable named item that represents the current item in the array.
- of items: Specifies the array or iterable you want to iterate over.
- element: The HTML element you want to repeat for each item in the array.

- {{ item }}: An example of displaying the current item using interpolation.

Common Use Cases for *ngFor:

*ngFor is a versatile directive that can be used in a variety of scenarios. Here are some common use cases:

- **Displaying a List of Products:** Create a list of product cards from an array of product data.

```
    <div *ngFor="let product of products" class="product-
card">
  <h2>{{ product.name }}</h2>
  <p>{{ product.description }}</p>
  <p>Price: ${{ product.price }}</p>
</div>
```

- **Creating a Table of Data:** Generate table rows from an array of data.

```
    <table>
  <thead>
    <tr>
      <th>Name</th>
      <th>Description</th>
      <th>Price</th>
    </tr>
  </thead>
  <tbody>
    <tr *ngFor="let product of products">
      <td>{{ product.name }}</td>
      <td>{{ product.description }}</td>
      <td>{{ product.price }}</td>
    </tr>
  </tbody>
</table>
```

- **Creating a Navigation Menu:** Generate navigation links from an array of menu items.

```
    <ul>
  <li *ngFor="let menuItem of menuItems">
    <a href="{{ menuItem.url }}">{{ menuItem.label }}</a>
  </li>
```

```
</ul>
```

Accessing Index, First, Last, Even, and Odd: Getting More Context

The *ngFor directive provides access to several other useful properties that give you more context about the current item in the array:

- **index:** The index of the current item (starting at 0).
- **first:** A boolean value indicating whether the current item is the first item in the array.
- **last:** A boolean value indicating whether the current item is the last item in the array.
- **even:** A boolean value indicating whether the current item's index is even.
- **odd:** A boolean value indicating whether the current item's index is odd.

To access these properties, you can use the let keyword to declare local variables:

```
    <li *ngFor="let item of items; let i = index; let
isFirst = first; let isLast = last; let isEven = even; let
isOdd = odd">
  {{ i + 1 }}. {{ item }} (First: {{ isFirst }}, Last: {{
isLast }}, Even: {{ isEven }}, Odd: {{ isOdd }})
</li>
```

Example: Styling List Items Based on Index

```
    <ul>
  <li *ngFor="let item of items; let i = index"
      [class.even]="i % 2 === 0"
      [class.odd]="i % 2 !== 0">
    {{ item }}
  </li>
</ul>
```

In this example, we're using the index property to add the even class to even-numbered list items and the odd class to odd-numbered list items. This results in a list where alternating items have different background colors.

Performance Considerations: The trackBy Function

When Angular re-renders a list, it needs to determine which items have changed so that it can update the DOM efficiently. By default, Angular uses object identity to track changes. However, this can be inefficient if you're working with large lists or if your data is frequently updated.

To improve performance, you can use the trackBy function to tell Angular how to uniquely identify each item in the array. The trackBy function should return a unique identifier for each item.

Syntax:

```
<li *ngFor="let item of items; trackBy: trackByFn">
{{ item }}
</li>
```

Example: Using the trackBy Function

```
// my-component.component.ts
import { Component } from '@angular/core';

@Component({
  selector: 'app-my-component',
  templateUrl: './my-component.component.html',
  styleUrls: ['./my-component.component.css']
})
export class MyComponent {
  items = [{ id: 1, name: 'Item 1' }, { id: 2, name: 'Item 2' }, { id: 3, name: 'Item 3' }];

  trackByFn(index: number, item: any): number {
    return item.id; // Use the item's id as the unique identifier
  }
}
```

```
<!-- my-component.component.html -->
<ul>
  <li *ngFor="let item of items; trackBy: trackByFn">{{item.name}}</li>
</ul>
```

In this example, the trackByFn() method returns the id of the current item. Angular will then use the id to track changes in the list.

Personal Insight: I've seen significant performance improvements in large lists by using the trackBy function. It's a simple but powerful optimization technique.

Why Is let item of items So Important?

Many new Angular developers try to skip the let item part and just use *ngFor="items". This won't work. The let item part declares a *template input variable*. It says, "For each cycle through this loop, create a variable called item that represents the current object". Without that, you have no way to refer to the current object in the template.

Conclusion: Your List-Building Powerhouse

*ngFor is an essential tool for creating dynamic lists, tables, and other data-driven interfaces in Angular. By mastering *ngFor and its related features, you can display collections of data with ease and create engaging user experiences. You now wield the power to dynamically generate content,

6.4 [ngClass]: Dynamic CSS Classes- Shaping the View with Style

We've seen how structural directives like *ngIf and *ngFor can change the structure of the DOM. Now, let's explore how attribute directives can change the appearance of elements. [ngClass] is your tool for dynamically adding or removing CSS classes from an element, allowing you to style it based on the state of your application. Think of [ngClass] as your style chameleon, adapting its appearance to the current context.

Beyond Static Styling: Reacting to the Application State

In traditional HTML and CSS, styling is typically static. You define the CSS classes for an element, and those classes remain unchanged. [ngClass] allows you to break free from this static approach and create elements that adapt their styling based on dynamic conditions.

The Mechanics of [ngClass]: Associating Styles with Conditions

[ngClass] works by evaluating expressions that determine whether a specific CSS class should be applied to an element. If the expression evaluates to true, the class is added. If the expression evaluates to false, the class is removed. This allows you to create elements that respond to changes in your application's data and logic.

The Syntax: Objects and Arrays are Your Allies

The [ngClass] directive uses two primary syntaxes for defining the classes to add or remove:

1. **Object Syntax (Most Common):** An object where the keys are CSS class names, and the values are boolean expressions.

```
<element [ngClass]="{ 'class-name': expression
}">Content</element>
```

2. **Array Syntax:** An array of CSS class names. Classes in the array are always applied; conditional logic is not directly supported in this syntax.

```
<element [ngClass]="['class1',
'class2']">Content</element>
```

Key Components:

- [ngClass]: The dynamic CSS class directive.
- 'class-name': The name of the CSS class you want to add or remove.
- expression: A TypeScript expression that evaluates to a boolean value (true or false).
- ['class1', 'class2']: An array of CSS class names.

Common Use Cases for [ngClass]}:

[ngClass] is a versatile directive that can be used in a variety of scenarios. Here are some common use cases:

- **Highlighting Active Navigation Links:** Add a "active" class to the currently selected navigation link.

```
// my-component.component.ts
import { Component } from '@angular/core';

@Component({
  selector: 'app-my-component',
```

```
  templateUrl: './my-component.component.html',
  styleUrls: ['./my-component.component.css']
})
export class MyComponent {
  activeRoute: string = '/home';
}
```

```html
    <!-- my-component.component.html -->
<ul>
  <li><a routerLink="/home" [ngClass]="{ 'active':
activeRoute === '/home' }">Home</a></li>
  <li><a routerLink="/about" [ngClass]="{ 'active':
activeRoute === '/about' }">About</a></li>
  <li><a routerLink="/contact" [ngClass]="{ 'active':
activeRoute === '/contact' }">Contact</a></li>
</ul>
```

- **Displaying Validation Errors:** Add an "error" class to an input field when it contains invalid data.

```html
    <input type="text" [(ngModel)]="name" [ngClass]="{
'error': name === '' }">
```

- **Styling List Items Based on Status:** Apply different styles to list items based on their status (e.g., "completed," "pending," "in progress").

```html
    <li *ngFor="let task of tasks" [ngClass]="{
'completed': task.isCompleted, 'pending': !task.isCompleted
}">
  {{ task.description }}
</li>
```

- **Alternating Row Colors in a Table:** Style even and odd rows differently for improved readability. (While CSS can now easily handle this, [ngClass] still works!)

```html
    <tr *ngFor="let item of items; let i = index"
[ngClass]="{ 'even': i % 2 === 0, 'odd': i % 2 !== 0 }">
  <td>{{ item.name }}</td>
  <td>{{ item.value }}</td>
</tr>
```

Mixing and Matching: Combining Multiple Classes

You can combine multiple classes using both the object and array syntax. This gives you a lot of flexibility in how you style your elements.

Example: Combining Static and Dynamic Classes

```
<div class="base-style" [ngClass]="{ 'highlighted':
isHighlighted, 'bold': isBold }">
  Content
</div>
```

In this example, the base-style class will always be applied to the <div> element, while the highlighted and bold classes will be added or removed based on the values of the isHighlighted and isBold properties, respectively.

Personal Insight: I've found [ngClass] to be invaluable for creating responsive and adaptable user interfaces. It allows me to easily change the appearance of elements based on the state of my application, without having to write complex JavaScript code.

A Word on Performance:

While [ngClass] is powerful, it's important to use it judiciously. Avoid using [ngClass] to dynamically apply a large number of classes, as this can impact performance. If you need to apply a large number of styles, it's often better to use [ngStyle] instead.

Conclusion: Your Styling Swiss Army Knife

[ngClass] is a powerful tool that allows you to dynamically add or remove CSS classes from elements based on the state of your Angular applications. By mastering [ngClass], you can create responsive, adaptable, and visually appealing user interfaces. You now have a versatile tool to shape the appearance of your application, making it truly reflect the dynamic nature of your data and logic. It's like having a styling Swiss Army knife right at your fingertips!

6.5 [ngStyle]: Dynamic Inline Styles- Direct Manipulation of Visual Appearance

We've explored how [ngClass] enables you to toggle CSS classes, applying pre-defined styles to your elements. But what if you need more granular control, directly manipulating the inline styles of an element? This is where [ngStyle] comes in, allowing you to dynamically set CSS style properties based on values in your component. Think of [ngStyle] as your direct line to visual customization, giving you pixel-perfect control over the look and feel of your application.

Beyond Predefined Styles: Fine-Grained Visual Control

While CSS classes offer a structured way to manage styles, there are times when you need to set specific style properties directly. This is often the case when you need to:

- Dynamically set sizes (e.g., width, height, font-size).
- Control colors based on data values.
- Adjust positioning based on calculations.
- React to dynamic layout changes.

The Mechanics of [ngStyle]: Directly Manipulating Inline Styles

[ngStyle] works by allowing you to bind a JavaScript object to the style attribute of an HTML element. The keys of the object represent CSS style properties, and the values represent the values you want to assign to those properties.

The Syntax: An Object of Style Rules

The [ngStyle] directive uses an object syntax to define the styles to apply:

```
<element [ngStyle]="{ 'style-property': expression }">Content</element>
```

Key Components:

- [ngStyle]: The dynamic inline style directive.

- 'style-property': The name of the CSS style property you want to set (e.g., 'color', 'fontSize', 'backgroundColor', 'width', 'height', 'transform'). Note that you should use camelCase for style names (e.g., backgroundColor instead of background-color).
- expression: A TypeScript expression that evaluates to the value you want to assign to the style property. This expression can be any valid JavaScript expression, including a property name, a function call, or a more complex calculation.

Common Use Cases for [ngStyle]:

[ngStyle] is a versatile directive that can be used in a variety of scenarios. Here are some common use cases:

- **Dynamically Setting Text Color:** Change the color of text based on the value of a property in your component.

```typescript
// my-component.component.ts
import { Component } from '@angular/core';

@Component({
  selector: 'app-my-component',
  templateUrl: './my-component.component.html',
  styleUrls: ['./my-component.component.css']
})
export class MyComponent {
  textColor: string = 'blue';
}
```

```html
<!-- my-component.component.html -->
<p [ngStyle]="{ 'color': textColor }">This is some text.</p>
```

- **Dynamically Setting Font Size:** Change the font size of text based on the value of a property.

```typescript
// my-component.component.ts
import { Component } from '@angular/core';

@Component({
  selector: 'app-my-component',
  templateUrl: './my-component.component.html',
  styleUrls: ['./my-component.component.css']
})
export class MyComponent {
```

```
    fontSize: number = 16;
}
```

```html
    <!-- my-component.component.html -->
<p [ngStyle]="{ 'font-size': fontSize + 'px' }">This is some
text.</p>
```

- **Dynamically Setting Background Color:** Change the background color of an element based on a condition.

```html
    <div [ngStyle]="{ 'background-color': isHighlighted ?
'yellow' : 'white' }">
  Content
</div>
```

- **Creating a Progress Bar:** Dynamically set the width of a progress bar based on the current progress value.

```html
    <div class="progress-bar" [ngStyle]="{ 'width':
progress + '%' }"></div>
```

- **Dynamically Setting the Opacity:** Create a fade-in or fade-out effect by dynamically setting the opacity of an element.

Best Practices:

- **Use Camel Case:** Use camel case for style property names in your JavaScript object (e.g., backgroundColor, fontSize, marginLeft).
- **Include Units:** Always include units for numeric values (e.g., '16px', '50%', '2em').
- **Combine with CSS Classes:** Use [ngStyle] in conjunction with CSS classes to maintain a consistent styling approach. Use classes for static styling and [ngStyle] for dynamic adjustments.

Personal Insight: I find [ngStyle] incredibly useful for creating dynamic visualizations and interactive elements. It gives me the control I need to fine-tune the appearance of my applications. However, I try to use it sparingly, as it can make your templates more difficult to read if overused. CSS classes are generally better for managing overall styling.

A Word on Security

As with other data binding techniques, be careful when using [ngStyle] to display data from external sources, as it can be vulnerable to CSS injection attacks. Always sanitize user input before displaying it in the template.

Choosing Between [ngClass] and [ngStyle]

When should you use [ngClass] and when should you use [ngStyle]?

- **Use [ngClass]** when you want to apply a set of predefined styles based on a condition.
- **Use [ngStyle]** when you need to set specific style properties directly.

In general, it's best to use CSS classes whenever possible, as they provide a more structured and maintainable approach to styling. Use [ngStyle] only when you need more fine-grained control over the appearance of your elements.

Conclusion: Painting with Code

[ngStyle] is a powerful tool that allows you to dynamically set the inline styles of elements based on the state of your Angular applications. By mastering [ngStyle], you can create highly customized and visually appealing user interfaces. You now have the ability to directly paint with code, transforming your application's appearance with precision and finesse. You are now a visual artist, directly shaping the look and feel of your application!

6.6 Example: Styling a List- A Symphony of Directives

We've explored the individual power of *ngIf, *ngFor, [ngClass], and [ngStyle]. Now, let's bring them together in a practical example to showcase their combined power: dynamically styling a list of items. This exercise will demonstrate how you can use these directives to create a visually appealing and informative user interface that responds to the underlying data. Think of this as composing a symphony, where each directive plays its part to create a harmonious whole.

From Isolated Techniques to a Cohesive Experience

Styling a list is a common task in web development. By combining the power of structural and attribute directives, we can create lists that are not only functional but also visually engaging.

The Requirements:

Our styled list will have the following features:

- A list of items displayed using *ngFor.
- Alternating row colors for improved readability, using [ngClass].
- Different styles applied to completed and pending tasks, again using [ngClass].
- Dynamic font sizes based on item priority, using [ngStyle].

Step-by-Step Implementation:

1. **Define the Component's Data:** In your component's TypeScript file (e.g., my-component.component.ts), define an array of items with properties for description, completed status, and priority:

```
import { Component } from '@angular/core';

@Component({
  selector: 'app-my-component',
  templateUrl: './my-component.component.html',
  styleUrls: ['./my-component.component.css']
})
export class MyComponent {
  tasks = [
    { description: 'Grocery Shopping', isCompleted: true,
priority: 2 },
    { description: 'Laundry', isCompleted: false, priority: 1
},
    { description: 'Pay Bills', isCompleted: false, priority:
3 },
    { description: 'Book Appointment', isCompleted: true,
priority: 1 }
  ];
}
```

Here, tasks is the array, and each item is an object with a description, isCompleted boolean, and priority number.

2. **Create the HTML Template:** In your component's HTML template (e.g., my-component.component.html), use *ngFor, [ngClass], and [ngStyle] to style the list items:

```
  <ul>
<li *ngFor="let task of tasks; let i = index"
    [ngClass]="{ 'completed': task.isCompleted, 'pending':
!task.isCompleted, 'even': i % 2 === 0, 'odd': i % 2 !== 0 }"
    [ngStyle]="{ 'font-size': task.priority * 4 + 'px' }">
  {{ task.description }}
</li>
</ul>
```

Explanation:

- *ngFor="let task of tasks; let i = index": This iterates over the tasks array, assigning the current task to the task variable and the index to the i variable.
- [ngClass]="{ 'completed': task.isCompleted, 'pending': !task.isCompleted, 'even': i % 2 === 0, 'odd': i % 2 !== 0 }": This adds the completed class if the task.isCompleted property is true, the pending class if it's false, the even class if the index is even, and the odd class if the index is odd.
- [ngStyle]="{ 'font-size': task.priority * 4 + 'px' }": This sets the font-size style property to a value based on the task.priority property.

3. **Define the CSS Classes:** In your component's CSS file (e.g., my-component.component.css), define the CSS classes used in the template:

```
  ul {
list-style-type: none; /* Remove bullet points */
padding: 0;
}

li {
  padding: 10px;
  margin-bottom: 5px;
}

.even {
  background-color: #f0f0f0; /* Light gray for even rows */
}

.odd {
```

```
    background-color: #ffffff; /* White for odd rows */
}

.completed {
    color: green; /* Green for completed tasks */
    text-decoration: line-through;
}

.pending {
    color: red; /* Red for pending tasks */
}
```

Analysis: Decoding the Directive Symphony

Let's analyze how these directives work together:

- *ngFor: Generates a list item (<li>) for each task in the tasks array, creating the basic structure of the list.
- [ngClass]: Dynamically applies CSS classes to each list item based on the task's completed status and its index, creating alternating row colors and visually distinguishing completed tasks from pending tasks.
- [ngStyle]: Dynamically sets the font size of each list item based on the task's priority, visually emphasizing higher-priority tasks.

Why This Approach is Powerful:

- **Data-Driven Styling:** The styling of the list is directly tied to the data in your component, making it easy to update the appearance of the list by simply changing the data.
- **Code Reusability:** The same styling logic can be applied to different lists throughout your application, promoting code reuse and consistency.
- **Readability:** The combination of directives and CSS classes makes the styling logic easy to understand and maintain.

Personal Insight: This example is a great illustration of how directives can work together to create a visually appealing and informative user interface. It shows how you can use Angular to go beyond basic HTML and create truly dynamic and engaging experiences.

Beyond the Basics: Enhancing the Styled List

Here are some ideas for enhancing the styled list example:

- Add a checkbox to each list item to allow the user to mark tasks as complete.
- Add a form to allow the user to add new tasks to the list.
- Allow the user to sort the list by priority, due date, or other criteria.
- Use property binding to display a tooltip with additional information about each task.

Important Considerations:

- **Maintainability:** While inline styles can be useful in some cases, it's generally best to use CSS classes for most of your styling. This makes your code easier to read and maintain.
- **Performance:** Be mindful of the number of expressions you use in your templates, as they can impact performance.

Conclusion: Conducting the Directive Orchestra

This example demonstrates the power of combining structural and attribute directives to create dynamic and visually appealing lists. By understanding how these directives work together, you can create highly customized and engaging user interfaces that respond to the specific needs of your application. You have now learned to conduct the directive orchestra, creating beautiful and responsive interfaces!

Chapter 7: Pipes: Transforming Data - Polishing Your Data Presentation

We've learned how to display data in our Angular templates using data binding. But what if you need to transform that data before displaying it? What if you need to format a date, convert a number to a currency, or change the case of a string? This is where **pipes** come in. Think of pipes as filters that you apply to your data to transform it into a more presentable format.

What Are Pipes? Adding Finishing Touches

Pipes are simple functions that accept an input value and return a transformed output value. They are used in Angular templates to format and transform data before it is displayed to the user. Pipes allow you to keep your component logic clean and focused on data retrieval and manipulation, while leaving the presentation details to the template. Pipes add elegance and clarity to your templates.

Key Characteristics of Pipes:

- **Data Transformation:** Pipes transform data from one format to another.
- **Template-Specific:** Pipes are used in Angular templates to format data before it is displayed.
- **Reusability:** Pipes can be reused throughout your application, promoting code reuse and consistency.
- **Chaining:** Pipes can be chained together to perform multiple transformations on a single value.
- **Extensibility:** Angular provides a way to create custom pipes, allowing you to extend the data transformation capabilities of your application.

7.1 What are Pipes?- Data Transformation for Elegant Presentation

We've explored components and directives, the foundational building blocks and modifiers of our Angular world. Now, let's add another powerful tool to your arsenal: pipes. Pipes are elegant functions that transform data for display in your templates, allowing you to present information in a user-friendly and consistent manner. Think of pipes as your personal data stylist, ensuring that your data always looks its best.

Beyond Raw Data: Crafting a Polished Presentation

Raw data, often retrieved from APIs or databases, rarely presents itself in the ideal format for display. Dates might be in a database format, numbers might need currency symbols, and text might require case transformations. Pipes are your solution for seamlessly bridging this gap between raw data and polished presentation.

What Do Pipes Actually Do?

At their core, pipes are functions that accept an input value and return a transformed output value. They don't change the underlying data; they simply create a formatted version for display in your templates. It's all about the presentation layer.

Key Characteristics of Pipes:

- **Data Transformation:** Pipes transform data from one format to another, enhancing its readability and usability.
- **Template-Centric:** Pipes are designed specifically for use in Angular templates, keeping your component logic clean and focused.
- **Reusability:** Pipes are reusable throughout your application, promoting consistency and reducing code duplication. You can create a pipe once and use it in multiple templates.
- **Declarative Approach:** Pipes provide a declarative way to transform data, making your templates easier to read and understand. You simply declare the transformation you want to perform, and Angular handles the rest.
- **Chaining:** Pipes can be chained together to perform multiple transformations on a single value, creating complex formatting pipelines.
- **Customizable:** Angular provides a set of built-in pipes, but you can also create your own custom pipes to handle specific data transformation requirements.

Why Are Pipes Important?

- **Improved Template Readability:** Pipes move data transformation logic out of the template and into reusable functions, making your templates cleaner and easier to understand. No more complex JavaScript expressions cluttering your HTML!

- **Enhanced Code Reusability:** You can reuse pipes throughout your application, ensuring that data is formatted consistently across different templates.
- **Reduced Component Complexity:** Pipes allow you to keep your component logic focused on data retrieval and manipulation, rather than presentation details.
- **Simplified Testing:** Pipes are easier to test because they are self-contained and have well-defined inputs and outputs.
- **Improved Maintainability:** Pipes make your code easier to maintain because data transformation logic is centralized in pipes, rather than scattered throughout your templates.

The Syntax: The Mighty Pipe Character (|)

To use a pipe in your template, you use the pipe operator (|), followed by the name of the pipe:

```
{{ value | pipeName }}
```

Passing Arguments to Pipes: Fine-Tuning the Transformation

Many pipes accept arguments that allow you to customize the transformation process. You can pass arguments to pipes using a colon (:), followed by the argument value:

```
{{ value | pipeName:argument1:argument2 }}
```

Behind the Scenes: How Angular Processes Pipes

When Angular encounters a pipe in your template, it performs the following steps:

1. **Retrieves the Pipe Instance:** Angular retrieves an instance of the specified pipe from its dependency injection container.
2. **Calls the transform() Method:** Angular calls the transform() method of the pipe, passing in the input value and any arguments.
3. **Displays the Transformed Value:** Angular displays the transformed value returned by the transform() method in the template.

Personal Insight: I used to write complex JavaScript expressions directly in my Angular templates to format data. This made my templates difficult to read and maintain. Once I discovered pipes, I was able to move all of that logic into reusable functions, making my templates much cleaner and easier to understand.

Beyond the Built-In: The Power of Custom Pipes

Angular provides a powerful set of built-in pipes for common data transformation tasks. However, you'll often encounter situations where you need to create your own custom pipes to handle specific data transformation requirements. This is where the true power of pipes comes into play.

Coming Up Next: Exploring Built-In and Custom Pipes

In the following sections, we'll explore some of the most commonly used built-in Angular pipes, including:

- DatePipe: Formatting dates.
- CurrencyPipe: Formatting currencies.
- UpperCasePipe and LowerCasePipe: Transforming text case.

We'll also provide a basic introduction to creating your own custom pipes, allowing you to tailor the data transformation capabilities of your application to your specific needs.

Conclusion: Elevating Your Data's Presentation

Pipes are powerful tools that allow you to transform data in your Angular templates, making your code easier to read, maintain, and test. By mastering pipes, you can create highly customized and visually appealing user interfaces that present your data in the best possible light. You now have the ability to take raw, unrefined data and turn it into a polished, presentable form, adding the final touches that elevate your application to the next level! You are now the master of data styling!

7.2 DatePipe: Formatting Dates- A Timeless Transformation

We've explored the general concept of pipes, and now it's time to delve into one of the most frequently used built-in pipes: DatePipe. Raw date information from databases or APIs can be cryptic and unreadable to users. Think of DatePipe as your translator, converting these machine-readable dates into human-friendly formats, allowing you to present time with style and clarity.

Beyond Raw Values: Crafting Readable Date Representations

Dates are a fundamental data type in many applications, but they often require formatting to be displayed in a way that is both understandable and visually appealing. DatePipe provides a powerful and flexible way to format dates according to a variety of predefined formats, or even your own custom patterns.

The Mechanics of DatePipe: Translating Dates into Readable Strings

DatePipe works by accepting a date value (either a Date object, a number representing milliseconds since the Unix epoch, or a string that can be parsed as a date) and a format string. It then uses the format string to generate a string representation of the date.

The Syntax: The Date Value and the Format String

To use DatePipe, you simply pipe the date value to the date pipe, followed by a colon (:) and the format string:

```
{{ dateValue | date:formatString }}
```

Key Components:

- dateValue: The date value you want to format. This can be a Date object, a number representing milliseconds since the Unix epoch, or a string that can be parsed as a date.
- date: The DatePipe's name.
- formatString: A string that specifies how the date should be formatted. This can be a predefined format string or a custom format string.

Predefined Format Strings: Quick and Easy Formatting

Angular provides a set of predefined format strings that cover most common date formatting needs. These format strings are easy to use and provide a consistent look and feel across your application.

Common Predefined Format Strings:

- 'short': Short date and time format (e.g., 6/15/24, 9:03 AM).
- 'medium': Medium date and time format (e.g., Jun 15, 2024, 9:03:01 AM).
- 'long': Long date and time format (e.g., June 15, 2024 at 9:03:01 AM PDT).
- 'full': Full date and time format (e.g., Saturday, June 15, 2024 at 9:03:01 AM Pacific Daylight Time).
- 'shortDate': Short date format (e.g., 6/15/24).
- 'mediumDate': Medium date format (e.g., Jun 15, 2024).
- 'longDate': Long date format (e.g., June 15, 2024).
- 'fullDate': Full date format (e.g., Saturday, June 15, 2024).
- 'shortTime': Short time format (e.g., 9:03 AM).
- 'mediumTime': Medium time format (e.g., 9:03:01 AM).
- 'longTime': Long time format (e.g., 9:03:01 AM PDT).
- 'fullTime': Full time format (e.g., 9:03:01 AM Pacific Daylight Time).

Example: Displaying a Date Using Predefined Format Strings

```typescript
// my-component.component.ts
import { Component } from '@angular/core';

@Component({
  selector: 'app-my-component',
  templateUrl: './my-component.component.html',
  styleUrls: ['./my-component.component.css']
})
export class MyComponent {
  myDate: Date = new Date();
}
```

content_copy download
Use code with caution.TypeScript

```html
<!-- my-component.component.html -->
<p>Short Date: {{ myDate | date:'short' }}</p>
<p>Medium Date: {{ myDate | date:'medium' }}</p>
<p>Long Date: {{ myDate | date:'long' }}</p>
```

Custom Format Strings: Tailoring the Date to Your Exact Needs

For more control over the date format, you can use custom format strings. Custom format strings allow you to specify the exact format you want to use, giving you complete control over the output.

Common Custom Format String Symbols:

- yyyy: Four-digit year (e.g., 2024).
- yy: Two-digit year (e.g., 24).
- MMMM: Full month name (e.g., June).
- MMM: Abbreviated month name (e.g., Jun).
- MM: Two-digit month (e.g., 06).
- M: Month (e.g., 6).
- dd: Two-digit day of the month (e.g., 15).
- d: Day of the month (e.g., 15).
- EEEE: Full day name (e.g., Saturday).
- EEE: Abbreviated day name (e.g., Sat).
- HH: Two-digit hour (24-hour clock) (e.g., 09).
- H: Hour (24-hour clock) (e.g., 9).
- hh: Two-digit hour (12-hour clock) (e.g., 09).
- h: Hour (12-hour clock) (e.g., 9).
- mm: Two-digit minute (e.g., 03).
- ss: Two-digit second (e.g., 01).
- a: AM/PM marker (e.g., AM).
- z: Timezone abbreviation (e.g., PDT).
- zzzz: Timezone name (e.g., Pacific Daylight Time).

Example: Displaying a Date Using a Custom Format String

```
<p>Custom Format: {{ myDate | date:'yyyy-MM-dd HH:mm:ss' }}</p>
```

This will display the date in the following format: 2024-06-15 09:03:01.

Personal Insight: I used to struggle with date formatting in JavaScript. The DatePipe makes it so much easier and more consistent. I highly recommend using custom format strings to ensure that your dates are displayed in a way that is both user-friendly and consistent with your application's design.

A Word on Time Zones:

The DatePipe uses the user's local timezone by default. You can specify a different timezone by passing a timezone string as the third argument to the pipe:

```
<p>Date in UTC: {{ myDate | date:'medium':'UTC' }}</p>
```

Conclusion: Presenting Time with Style

DatePipe is an essential tool for formatting dates in your Angular applications. By mastering DatePipe and its various options, you can present time with style, clarity, and consistency. You now have the power to transform raw date values into human-friendly formats, ensuring that your users always see dates in a way that is both understandable and visually appealing. You are now a master of time presentation!

7.3 CurrencyPipe: Formatting Currencies- Making Monetary Values Understandable

We've conquered date formatting, and now it's time to tackle another common data presentation challenge: currency formatting. Raw numerical price values are rarely sufficient for a user-friendly interface. The CurrencyPipe is your financial translator, converting plain numbers into beautifully formatted currency strings, allowing you to present prices and monetary values with clarity and precision. Think of it as your key to international finance, rendering monetary values across the globe.

Beyond Raw Numbers: Communicating Value Effectively

Presenting currency information in a consistent and easily understandable way is critical for e-commerce applications, financial dashboards, and any other application that deals with monetary values. CurrencyPipe ensures that your users can quickly and easily understand the value of your products, services, or transactions.

The Mechanics of CurrencyPipe: Transforming Numbers into Currency Strings

CurrencyPipe works by accepting a number value and a set of formatting options. It then uses these options to generate a string representation of the number, including the appropriate currency symbol or code, the correct number of decimal places, and the appropriate thousands separator.

The Syntax: Value, Currency, and Style

To use CurrencyPipe, you simply pipe the number value to the currency pipe, followed by a colon (:) and the formatting options:

```
{{ numberValue |
currency:currencyCode:'symbol|code':digitsInfo }}
```

Key Components:

- numberValue: The number value you want to format as a currency.
- currency: The name of the CurrencyPipe.
- currencyCode: The ISO 4217 currency code (e.g., 'USD', 'EUR', 'GBP', 'JPY'). This is a *required* argument.
- 'symbol|code': Determines whether to display the currency symbol (e.g., $, €, £) or the currency code (e.g., USD, EUR, GBP). This is an *optional* argument; if omitted, the default is 'symbol'.
- digitsInfo: Specifies the minimum and maximum number of digits to use for the integer and fractional parts of the number. This is an *optional* argument; if omitted, the default is based on the locale. The format is {minIntegerDigits}.{minFractionDigits}-{maxFractionDigits}.

Understanding the Arguments: Fine-Tuning the Output

- **currencyCode:** The ISO 4217 currency code is a three-letter code that represents a specific currency (e.g., USD for United States Dollar, EUR for Euro, GBP for British Pound). You can find a complete list of currency codes at https://en.wikipedia.org/wiki/ISO_4217.
- **symbolDisplay:** This argument controls whether the currency symbol or the currency code is displayed.
    - 'symbol': Displays the currency symbol (e.g., $99.99).
    - 'code': Displays the currency code (e.g., USD 99.99).
- **digitsInfo:** This argument controls the number of digits used to format the number. It has the following format:
- ```
  {minIntegerDigits}.{minFractionDigits}-{maxFractionDigits}
  ```
  ```

content_copy download

Use code with caution.

- o minIntegerDigits: The minimum number of integer digits to use. If the number has fewer integer digits than specified, it will be padded with leading zeros. The default is 1.
- o minFractionDigits: The minimum number of fraction digits to use. If the number has fewer fraction digits than specified, it will be padded with trailing zeros. The default is based on the locale (usually 0-2).
- o maxFractionDigits: The maximum number of fraction digits to use. If the number has more fraction digits than specified, it will be rounded to the specified number of digits. The default is based on the locale (usually 0-2).

Example: Displaying Prices in Different Currencies and Formats

```
// my-component.component.ts
import { Component } from '@angular/core';

@Component({
  selector: 'app-my-component',
  templateUrl: './my-component.component.html',
  styleUrls: ['./my-component.component.css']
})
export class MyComponent {
  price: number = 1234.567;
}
```

```
<!-- my-component.component.html -->
<p>USD (Symbol): {{ price | currency:'USD' }}</p>
<p>EUR (Symbol, 2 Digits): {{ price |
currency:'EUR':'symbol':'1.2-2' }}</p>
<p>GBP (Code): {{ price | currency:'GBP':'code' }}</p>
<p>JPY (Symbol, 0 Digits): {{ price |
currency:'JPY':'symbol':'1.0-0' }}</p>
```

Output:

```
USD (Symbol): $1,234.57
EUR (Symbol, 2 Digits): €1,234.57
GBP (Code): GBP1,234.57
JPY (Symbol, 0 Digits): ¥1,235
```

Personal Insight: CurrencyPipe is an absolute must-have for any application that deals with monetary values. It ensures that prices are displayed in a way that is both accurate and visually appealing, improving the overall user experience.

A Note on Localization:

The CurrencyPipe is locale-aware, meaning that it will automatically format the currency according to the user's locale. This ensures that your application displays currencies correctly for users all over the world.

When to Use Currency Codes vs. Symbols:

Whether to use currency codes or symbols is largely a design decision. Symbols are generally more recognizable and user-friendly. However, in certain situations, currency codes may be more appropriate, such as when dealing with multiple currencies in a limited space.

Beyond the Basics: Customizing Currency Formatting

While CurrencyPipe provides a lot of flexibility, you may need to create your own custom pipe for more complex currency formatting requirements. For example, you might need to display a custom currency symbol or use a differentThousands separator. Creating custom pipes is easy in Angular!

Conclusion: Master of Monetary Presentation

CurrencyPipe is a powerful tool for formatting numbers as currencies in your Angular applications. By mastering CurrencyPipe and its various options, you can present prices and monetary values with clarity, precision, and cultural sensitivity. You now have the power to transform raw numerical values into beautifully formatted currency strings, ensuring that your users always understand the value of your products, services, or transactions. You are now a financial presentation expert!

7.4 UpperCasePipe and LowerCasePipe: Text Case-Enforcing Consistent Style

While they might seem simple, the UpperCasePipe and LowerCasePipe are invaluable tools for maintaining consistency in your application's text. Think of these pipes as your text stylists, ensuring that headings, labels, and other textual elements adhere to a consistent style, no matter the source of the data.

Beyond Data Transformation: Enforcing Style Guidelines

Data can come from various sources – user input, external APIs, databases – and the case of the text might not always be what you desire for your application's UI. These pipes are simple yet effective for ensuring stylistic conformity.

The Mechanics: Simple Case Conversions

These pipes perform very straightforward operations:

- UpperCasePipe: Converts all characters in a string to uppercase.
- LowerCasePipe: Converts all characters in a string to lowercase.

The core functionality is simple, but the implications for consistency are powerful.

The Syntax: Minimal and Direct

The syntax is as simple as it gets. You simply pipe the string value to the appropriate pipe:

```
{{ stringValue | uppercase }}
{{ stringValue | lowercase }}
```

Example: Formatting Text in Headings and Labels

```
// my-component.component.ts
import { Component } from '@angular/core';

@Component({
  selector: 'app-my-component',
  templateUrl: './my-component.component.html',
  styleUrls: ['./my-component.component.css']
})
export class MyComponent {
  pageTitle: string = 'product details';
  userName: string = 'johnDoe123';
}
```

```
<!-- my-component.component.html -->
<h1>{{ pageTitle | uppercase }}</h1>
<p>Welcome, {{ userName | lowercase }}!</p>
```

Common Use Cases for UpperCasePipe and LowerCasePipe:

- **Headings and Titles:** Ensuring that headings and titles are consistently displayed in uppercase, regardless of how they are stored in the database.
- **Labels:** Converting labels to lowercase for a more consistent and modern look.
- **Usernames and Email Addresses:** Converting usernames and email addresses to lowercase for case-insensitive comparisons.
- **Displaying Status Messages:** Standardizing the case of status messages for consistency.
- **Search Queries (Less Common):** While it's more common to normalize the data *before* searching, you *could* use these pipes to change the search terms entered by the user for a case-insensitive search.

Beyond the Obvious: Thinking Strategically About Text Case

While these pipes are easy to use, it's important to think strategically about how you use them. Consider the following:

- **Consistency:** Be consistent in your use of uppercase and lowercase throughout your application. Choose a style guide and stick to it.
- **Accessibility:** Consider the accessibility implications of your text case choices. All-uppercase text can be difficult to read for some users.
- **Search Engine Optimization (SEO):** Use appropriate text case for headings and titles to improve your application's SEO.

When To Normalize the Source Data

While these pipes can clean up text presentation, it's often best practice to normalize the data itself where possible. For example, usernames and email addresses should be saved in lowercase in your database to facilitate case-insensitive comparisons. You can use these pipes for display, but also consider data normalization as a separate step.

Personal Insight: I used to think that text case was a trivial matter, but I've learned that it can have a significant impact on the overall look and feel of your application. Using these pipes consistently can help you create a more professional and polished user interface.

Custom Implementations: When You Need More Control

You might want to create custom implementations for localized casing or to handle Unicode complexities. This is where custom pipes excel, allowing you to have granular control over the transformation.

Conclusion: Elevating Your Text Presentation

UpperCasePipe and LowerCasePipe are simple but powerful tools for maintaining consistency in your application's text. By mastering these pipes, you can create a more professional, polished, and user-friendly user interface. They provide the final, crucial touch that transforms your data from mere text into elegantly styled information. You are now a text style guru!

7.5 Custom Pipes (Basic Introduction)- Your Personalized Data Transformation Toolkit

We've explored the power of Angular's built-in pipes, but sometimes you need a transformation that's highly specific to your application. This is where custom pipes come into play, giving you the ability to create your own personalized data transformation toolkit. Think of custom pipes as your tailor-made data styling solutions, allowing you to shape your data's presentation to meet your precise needs.

Beyond the Standard: Creating Specialized Transformations

Angular's built-in pipes provide a solid foundation for common data transformation tasks. However, they can't cover every possible scenario. Custom pipes allow you to extend Angular's data transformation capabilities and create reusable functions that are tailored to your specific application's requirements.

The Mechanics of Creating Custom Pipes: A Step-by-Step Guide

Creating a custom pipe involves the following steps:

1. **Create a TypeScript Class:** Create a new TypeScript class that will implement the custom pipe's logic. This class will contain the transform() method, which performs the data transformation.
2. **Implement the PipeTransform Interface:** Implement the PipeTransform interface from @angular/core. This interface defines the transform() method that your pipe must implement.
3. **Decorate the Class with @Pipe:** Decorate the class with the @Pipe decorator from @angular/core. This decorator tells Angular that the class is a pipe and specifies the name of the pipe.
4. **Implement the transform() Method:** Implement the transform() method, which accepts the input value and any arguments and returns the transformed value.
5. **Declare the Pipe in a Module:** Add the custom pipe to the declarations array of your application module (or a feature module). This makes the pipe available for use in your templates.

A Code Example: Creating a TruncatePipe

Let's create a custom pipe that truncates a string to a specified length and adds a trailing ellipsis (...). This is useful for displaying long strings in a limited space.

1. **Create the TruncatePipe Class:** Create a new file named truncate.pipe.ts and add the following code:

```typescript
// truncate.pipe.ts
import { Pipe, PipeTransform } from '@angular/core';

@Pipe({
  name: 'truncate' // This is the name you'll use in the template
})
export class TruncatePipe implements PipeTransform {
  transform(value: string, limit: number = 25, completeWords:
boolean = false, trail: string = '...'): string {
    if (!value) {
      return ''; // Return empty string if value is null or
undefined
    }

    if (completeWords) {
        limit = value.substring(0, limit).lastIndexOf(' ');
    }

    return value.length > limit ? value.substring(0, limit) +
trail : value;
```

```
    }
}
```

Explanation:

- import { Pipe, PipeTransform } from '@angular/core';: This imports the Pipe decorator and the PipeTransform interface from @angular/core.
- @Pipe({ name: 'truncate' }): This decorator tells Angular that the class is a pipe and specifies the name of the pipe as 'truncate'. This is the name you'll use in your templates to invoke the pipe.
- export class TruncatePipe implements PipeTransform { ... }: This defines the TruncatePipe class, which implements the PipeTransform interface.
- transform(value: string, limit: number = 25, completeWords: boolean = false, trail: string = '...'): string { ... }: This implements the transform() method, which accepts the input value (value), the maximum length (limit), a flag for word boundary truncation (completeWords) and a trailing string (trail). It returns the truncated string.
- if (!value) { return ''; }: Handles empty or null inputs.

2. **Declare the TruncatePipe in a Module:** Add the TruncatePipe to the declarations array of your application module (e.g., app.module.ts):

```
import { BrowserModule } from '@angular/platform-
browser';
import { NgModule } from '@angular/core';
import { AppComponent } from './app.component';
import { TruncatePipe } from './truncate.pipe'; // Import the
custom pipe

@NgModule({
  declarations: [
    AppComponent,
    TruncatePipe // Declare the custom pipe
  ],
  imports: [
    BrowserModule
  ],
  providers: [],
  bootstrap: [AppComponent]
})
export class AppModule { }
```

This step is crucial for Angular to recognize and use your custom pipe.

3. **Use the TruncatePipe in a Template:** You can now use the TruncatePipe in your templates:

```
<p>{{ longText | truncate }}</p>
<p>{{ longText | truncate: 50 }}</p>
<p>{{ longText | truncate: 30: true }}</p>
<p>{{ longText | truncate: 40: false: '[...]' }}</p>
```

In these examples, the TruncatePipe is used to truncate the longText string to different lengths.

Analyzing the TruncatePipe:

- **Customizable:** The TruncatePipe accepts arguments to control the maximum length, whether to truncate at word boundaries, and the trailing string to use. This makes the pipe highly customizable and reusable.
- **Handles Edge Cases:** The pipe handles edge cases such as null or undefined input values, ensuring that your application doesn't throw errors.
- **Maintains Readability:** The pipe keeps your templates clean and readable by encapsulating the truncation logic in a separate function.

Personal Insight: I find custom pipes incredibly valuable for creating reusable data transformations that are specific to my application's needs. They help me keep my templates clean and focused on presentation. I use custom pipes for everything from formatting phone numbers to displaying relative dates (e.g., "5 minutes ago").

Beyond Simple Text Transformations:

Custom pipes aren't limited to just text transformations. You can also create custom pipes to transform numbers, dates, objects, and any other data type.

When to Use a Custom Pipe (and When Not To)

It's tempting to create a custom pipe for every data transformation, but it's important to use them judiciously. Consider the following:

- **Reusability:** Will this transformation be used in multiple templates throughout your application? If not, it might be better to perform the transformation directly in the component.
- **Complexity:** Is the transformation complex? If so, a custom pipe can help to simplify your templates and improve readability.
- **Testability:** Is the transformation logic easy to test? If so, a custom pipe can make it easier to write unit tests for your data transformation code.

Conclusion: Crafting Your Data Transformation Toolkit

Creating custom pipes is a powerful way to extend Angular's data transformation capabilities and tailor them to your specific application's needs. By mastering custom pipes, you can create highly customized and visually appealing user interfaces that present your data in the best possible light. You now have the power to build your own personalized data transformation toolkit, making your Angular applications even more powerful and flexible! You are now a data transformation artisan!

Chapter 8: User Input and Forms - Gathering Information and Interacting with Users

We've covered how to display data and dynamically style your application. Now, it's time to learn how to gather information from users using forms. Forms are essential for creating interactive web applications that allow users to input data, submit requests, and interact with your application's logic.

Why are Forms Important?

Forms are the primary way users interact with your application, allowing them to:

- **Submit Data:** Collect information such as names, email addresses, and passwords.
- **Make Choices:** Allow users to select options from dropdown menus or radio buttons.
- **Control Application Behavior:** Provide controls for filtering data, configuring settings, and performing other actions.
- **Search for Information:** Enable users to search for specific data within your application.

Template-Driven vs. Reactive Forms: Two Approaches to Form Management

Angular provides two distinct approaches to working with forms:

- **Template-Driven Forms:** This approach relies on directives in the template to manage form controls and validation. It's a simpler approach that's well-suited for basic forms.
- **Reactive Forms:** This approach uses a more programmatic approach, defining form controls and validation in the component class. It's a more powerful and flexible approach that's well-suited for complex forms.

In this chapter, we'll focus on Template-Driven Forms to get you started with form handling in Angular. Reactive Forms will be tackled in a later, more advanced section.

8.1 Template-Driven Forms: An Overview- The Fast Track to Form Handling

While Angular provides two approaches to form handling – template-driven and reactive – template-driven forms offer a gentler learning curve and a more intuitive approach for simpler scenarios. Think of template-driven forms as the "express lane" for creating forms, allowing you to quickly gather user input and process it without getting bogged down in complex programmatic setup.

Beyond Basic Input: Making Forms an Integral Part of Your UI

Forms are not just about collecting data; they are a critical point of interaction between your application and its users. A well-designed form should be intuitive, easy to use, and provide clear feedback to the user. Template-driven forms, with their reliance on directives in the HTML template, allow you to create forms that seamlessly integrate with your application's UI.

Key Characteristics of Template-Driven Forms: Simplicity and Integration

- **Simplified Setup:** Template-driven forms require minimal setup in the component class. Most of the form logic is handled directly in the template, using directives.
- **Template-Centric Approach:** The form's structure, data binding, and validation are primarily defined within the HTML template.
- **Ideal for Basic Forms:** Template-driven forms are best suited for forms with a limited number of controls and straightforward validation requirements. Think contact forms, login forms, or simple data entry forms.
- **Two-Way Binding with [(ngModel)]:** Template-driven forms heavily rely on two-way binding with the [(ngModel)] directive to synchronize data between the form controls and the component properties. This simplifies the process of displaying and updating form data.
- **Automatic Tracking of Form State:** Angular automatically tracks the state of the form and its controls, making it easy to display validation errors and control the form's submission behavior.
- **FormsModule Dependency:** Template-driven forms require importing the FormsModule into your application module. This

module provides the necessary directives and services for working with template-driven forms.

The Essential Components of Template-Driven Forms: The Key Players

- **ngModel Directive: The Data Binder**

  The ngModel directive is the cornerstone of template-driven forms. It enables two-way binding between a form control (e.g., an input field, textarea, select box) and a property in your component. This means that changes made to the form control are automatically reflected in the component property, and vice versa. ngModel provides the crucial data link.

- **name Attribute: Identifying the Controls**

  Each form control must have a name attribute. This attribute is used by Angular to track the form controls and manage their state. The name is the control's unique identifier.

- **FormsModule: The Form Enabler**

  The FormsModule is the Angular module that provides the necessary directives and services for working with template-driven forms. You must import this module into your application module (or a feature module) to use template-driven forms. FormsModule brings the template features to life.

- **Template Variables: Accessing Form Elements**

  Template variables allow you to access form and control elements directly in the template. This is useful for displaying validation errors and controlling the form's submission behavior. Template variables allow you to check the form's status.

When to Choose Template-Driven Forms (and When to Consider Reactive Forms)

Template-driven forms are a great choice for:

- **Simple Forms:** Forms with a limited number of controls and basic validation requirements.

- **Rapid Prototyping:** Quickly creating forms for testing and demonstration purposes.
- **Learning Angular Forms:** Providing a gentle introduction to form handling in Angular.

However, for more complex scenarios, you should consider using reactive forms. Reactive forms offer more control, flexibility, and testability.

Key Reasons to Consider Reactive Forms:

- **Complex Validation:** When you need more sophisticated validation rules, such as custom validators or asynchronous validation.
- **Dynamic Forms:** When the structure of your form needs to change dynamically based on user input or other factors.
- **Unit Testing:** When you want to write comprehensive unit tests for your form logic.
- **Large Forms:** For very large forms, reactive forms can offer better performance.

Personal Insight: I often start with template-driven forms for simple forms, and then refactor to reactive forms if the complexity increases. This allows me to get up and running quickly and then add more control as needed.

A Simpler Alternative: Native HTML5 Forms

In simpler scenarios, you can consider using native HTML5 form features (e.g., the required attribute) without using Angular forms at all. For simple form capture, that may be a sufficient starting point.

Conclusion: Your Gateway to Form Handling

Template-driven forms provide a straightforward and intuitive way to create and manage forms in Angular applications. They're a great starting point for learning form handling in Angular and are well-suited for simpler forms with basic validation requirements. It's a great entry point to understand data gathering. You are now ready to embark on the journey of gathering user data!

8.2 Binding Inputs: ngModel in Action- Establishing the Two-Way Connection

We've laid the groundwork for understanding template-driven forms. Now, let's delve into the heart of data synchronization: the ngModel directive. Think of ngModel as the conductor of your form's data orchestra, ensuring that changes in the view (the input fields) are seamlessly reflected in the component's data model, and vice versa. It's the key to making your forms dynamic and responsive.

Beyond Static Values: Dynamic Synchronization with [(ngModel)]

In traditional HTML, input fields are static elements that hold values entered by the user. While you can access these values using JavaScript, you need to write code to manually update the view whenever the data changes and vice versa. ngModel automates this process, creating a two-way data binding between the input field and a component property.

The Mechanics of ngModel: The Two-Way Dance

ngModel works by establishing a two-way data binding between a form control and a property in your component's TypeScript class. This means that:

1. **Property Binding:** The value property of the input element is bound to the specified component property. This ensures that the input field initially displays the value of the component property.
2. **Event Binding:** The input event on the input element is bound to a function that updates the component property whenever the user changes the value in the input field. This ensures that the component property is always in sync with the input field.

The Syntax: The Banana in a Box - [(ngModel)]

To use ngModel, you simply add the [(ngModel)] directive to the input element, specifying the name of the component property you want to bind to. This syntax is often referred to as "banana in a box" due to its shape:

```
<input type="text" [(ngModel)]="componentProperty"
name="inputName">
```

Key Components:

- input (or other form element): The HTML input element you want to bind to (e.g., <input type="text">, <textarea>, <select>).
- [(ngModel)]="componentProperty": The two-way binding directive that binds the input element to the componentProperty in your component.
- name="inputName": The name of the input element. This is *required* for template-driven forms. It allows Angular to track the state of the form control and perform validation.

A Deeper Look at the name Attribute:

The name attribute isn't just a formality; it's crucial for Angular to manage the form correctly. Angular uses the name attribute to:

- **Register the control with the form:** Without a name, Angular won't know about the control.
- **Track the control's state:** This allows you to determine if the control has been modified (is "dirty"), if it has focus (is "touched"), and if it is valid.
- **Group controls (in reactive forms, but important to know):** The name is how form controls are grouped in a reactive form.

Example: Binding an Input Field to a Component Property

```
     // my-component.component.ts
import { Component } from '@angular/core';

@Component({
  selector: 'app-my-component',
  templateUrl: './my-component.component.html',
  styleUrls: ['./my-component.component.css']
})
export class MyComponent {
  name: string = '';
}


     <!-- my-component.component.html -->
<label for="nameInput">Name:</label>
<input type="text" id="nameInput" [(ngModel)]="name"
name="nameInput">
<p>You entered: {{ name }}</p>
```

In this example, the name property in the MyComponent class is bound to the <input> element using [(ngModel)]. When the user types in the input field, the name property is automatically updated, and the value is displayed below using interpolation.

Different Form Controls: Adapting to Different Input Types

ngModel can be used with a variety of form controls, including:

- <input type="text">
- <input type="number">
- <input type="email">
- <textarea>
- <select>
- <input type="checkbox">
- <input type="radio">

A Note on Checkboxes and Radio Buttons:

When using ngModel with checkboxes and radio buttons, the component property should be of type boolean (for checkboxes) or of the same type as the value attribute of the radio buttons.

Personal Insight: I initially found the [(ngModel)] syntax a little strange, but I quickly came to appreciate its power and simplicity. It's such a concise way to create two-way data bindings!

When to Use ngModel (and When to Consider Alternative Approaches)

ngModel is a great choice for many form scenarios, but it's not always the best option. Consider the following:

- **Complexity:** For very complex forms with a lot of custom logic, reactive forms may provide more control and flexibility.
- **Performance:** In some cases, ngModel can have a slight performance impact, especially with large forms.
- **Testability:** Reactive forms generally offer better testability.

Conclusion: Making the Data Connection

ngModel is a powerful directive that enables two-way binding between form controls and component properties in template-driven forms. By mastering ngModel, you can create dynamic and interactive forms with ease, simplifying the process of gathering user input and processing it in your application. You have now mastered the data connection, forging a seamless link between the user interface and your application's logic!

8.3 Handling Form Submission: Capturing and Processing User Data

We've learned how to create input fields and bind them to our component's data. Now, let's tackle the core purpose of most forms: capturing and processing user data. Think of handling form submission as receiving the baton in a relay race, taking the data from the user interface and passing it on to the next stage of your application's workflow.

Beyond Data Entry: Triggering Action and Logic

Forms are not just passive recipients of data; they are active triggers that initiate actions and drive your application's behavior. Submitting a form signals that the user has completed a set of inputs and is ready to proceed. This is your cue to validate the data, process it, and perform the appropriate action, whether it's saving data to a database, sending an email, or updating the user interface.

The Mechanics of Form Submission: Listening and Responding

Handling form submission involves the following steps:

1. **Creating a Form:** Constructing the HTML <form> element with the appropriate input fields and attributes.
2. **Binding to the ngSubmit Event:** Using event binding to listen for the ngSubmit event on the <form> element.
3. **Implementing the Submission Handler:** Defining a method in your component's TypeScript class to handle the form submission.
4. **Accessing the Form Data:** Retrieving the data entered by the user from the form controls.
5. **Preventing Default Behavior (Optional):** Preventing the browser from performing its default form submission behavior (e.g., reloading the page).
6. **Processing the Form Data:** Performing the necessary actions with the form data (e.g., validating the data, sending it to a server).

The Syntax: (ngSubmit) and the Submission Handler

To handle form submission, you use the (ngSubmit) event binding on the <form> element:

```
    <form (ngSubmit)="onSubmit()">
  <!-- Form controls go here -->
  <button type="submit">Submit</button>
</form>
```

Key Components:

- <form>: The HTML form element.
- (ngSubmit)="onSubmit()": The event binding that listens for the ngSubmit event and calls the onSubmit() method in your component.
- <button type="submit">: The submit button that triggers the ngSubmit event.

Preventing the Default Form Submission Behavior:

By default, submitting a form will cause the browser to reload the page. This is often undesirable in single-page applications (SPAs). To prevent this behavior, you can call the preventDefault() method on the event object passed to the submission handler:

```
    onSubmit(event: Event): void {
  event.preventDefault(); // Prevent page reload
  // Process the form data
}
```

Important: Always specify the type="submit" attribute on your submit button. This ensures that the button triggers the form submission.

Accessing the Form Data: The Power of ngModel

Since we are using template-driven forms, the primary way to access the data from your form is using the two-way binding with [(ngModel)] on each form control. This ensures that the data entered by the user is automatically synchronized with the corresponding properties in your component's TypeScript class.

Example: Handling Form Submission and Accessing the Data

```typescript
// my-component.component.ts
import { Component } from '@angular/core';

@Component({
  selector: 'app-my-component',
  templateUrl: './my-component.component.html',
  styleUrls: ['./my-component.component.css']
})
export class MyComponent {
  name: string = '';
  email: string = '';
  message: string = '';

  onSubmit(event: Event): void {
    event.preventDefault(); // Prevent page reload
    console.log('Form submitted!');
    console.log('Name:', this.name);
    console.log('Email:', this.email);
    console.log('Message:', this.message);

    // Perform further processing (e.g., send data to a
server)
  }
}
```

```html
<!-- my-component.component.html -->
<form (ngSubmit)="onSubmit($event)">
  <div>
    <label for="nameInput">Name:</label>
    <input type="text" id="nameInput" [(ngModel)]="name"
name="name" required>
  </div>
  <div>
    <label for="emailInput">Email:</label>
    <input type="email" id="emailInput" [(ngModel)]="email"
name="email" required>
  </div>
  <div>
    <label for="messageInput">Message:</label>
    <textarea id="messageInput" [(ngModel)]="message"
name="message" required></textarea>
  </div>
  <button type="submit">Submit</button>
</form>
```

In this example, the onSubmit() method is called when the form is submitted. The method prevents the default form submission behavior, logs a message

141

to the console, and displays the values of the name, email, and message properties. You can then perform further processing of the form data, such as sending it to a server.

Beyond the Basics: Advanced Form Submission Techniques

- **Validating the Form:** Before processing the form data, it's important to validate the data to ensure that it meets your application's requirements. We'll cover form validation in more detail in the next section.
- **Displaying Success/Error Messages:** After processing the form data, it's important to provide feedback to the user, such as displaying a success message or an error message.
- **Disabling the Submit Button:** To prevent the user from submitting the form multiple times, you can disable the submit button while the form is being processed.
- **Resetting the Form:** After the form has been submitted successfully, you can reset the form to clear the input fields.

Personal Insight: I always make sure to prevent the default form submission behavior in my Angular applications. It's a simple but important step that can significantly improve the user experience.

A Note on Server-Side Processing:

This section focuses on the client-side aspects of form submission. In a real-world application, you'll typically send the form data to a server for further processing. This often involves making an HTTP request to a backend API. We'll cover HTTP communication in more detail in a later chapter.

Conclusion: Completing the Form Cycle

Handling form submission is a crucial step in building interactive web applications. By mastering the techniques outlined in this section, you can capture user data, process it effectively, and provide feedback to the user.

8.4 Basic Form Validation: Guarding the Gates of Data Integrity

We've learned how to capture user input using forms and handle the form submission process. Now, let's focus on a critical aspect of form handling:

ensuring data quality through validation. Think of form validation as your security system, guarding the gates of your application and preventing invalid or malicious data from entering.

Beyond Data Collection: Ensuring Data Accuracy and Completeness

Form validation is the process of verifying that the data entered by the user meets certain criteria before it's submitted to your application. This is crucial for:

- **Preventing Errors:** Ensuring that the data is in the correct format (e.g., a valid email address, a number within a specific range).
- **Improving Data Quality:** Enforcing rules to ensure that the data is accurate and complete.
- **Protecting Your Application:** Preventing malicious input that could compromise your application's security.
- **Enhancing User Experience:** Providing clear and informative feedback to the user when they enter invalid data.

The Mechanics of Basic Form Validation: Leveraging HTML5 Attributes

Template-driven forms in Angular make it easy to perform basic form validation using standard HTML5 validation attributes. These attributes provide built-in validation rules that are automatically enforced by the browser and by Angular.

Common HTML5 Validation Attributes:

- **required:** Specifies that the input field must be filled out before the form can be submitted.
- minlength: Specifies the minimum length of the input value.
- maxlength: Specifies the maximum length of the input value.
- pattern: Specifies a regular expression that the input value must match. This allows very precise format control, such as phone numbers or specific license plate patterns.
- type="email": Specifies that the input field should contain a valid email address. This triggers built-in email format validation.
- type="number": Specifies that the input field should contain a valid number. This trigger built-in number formatting validation.
- min: Specifies the minimum value for a number input.
- max: Specifies the maximum value for a number input.

Example: Adding Validation Attributes to a Form

```
     <div>
  <label for="nameInput">Name:</label>
  <input type="text" id="nameInput" [(ngModel)]="name"
name="name" required minlength="3">
</div>
<div>
  <label for="emailInput">Email:</label>
  <input type="email" id="emailInput" [(ngModel)]="email"
name="email" required email>
</div>
<div>
  <label for="ageInput">Age:</label>
  <input type="number" id="ageInput" [(ngModel)]="age"
name="age" min="18" max="99">
</div>
```

In this example, we've added validation attributes to the name, email, and age input fields:

- The name field is required and must be at least 3 characters long.
- The email field is required and must contain a valid email address.
- The age field must be a number between 18 and 99.

Displaying Validation Errors: Giving the User Feedback

Adding validation attributes is only half the battle. You also need to display validation errors to the user, providing them with clear and informative feedback about what they need to fix. This improves the user experience and helps them to enter valid data.

Accessing Form Control Validation State: Template Variables to the Rescue

To display validation errors, you need to access the validation state of the form control. You can do this using template variables.

Creating a Template Variable:

To create a template variable for a form control, you use the #variableName="ngModel" syntax on the input element:

```
    <input type="text" id="nameInput" [(ngModel)]="name"
name="name" required minlength="3" #nameInput="ngModel">
```

In this example, we've created a template variable named nameInput that references the ngModel directive for the name input field.

Accessing Validation Properties:

Once you have a template variable, you can use it to access the following properties:

- valid: A boolean value indicating whether the form control is valid.
- invalid: A boolean value indicating whether the form control is invalid.
- errors: An object containing any validation errors. This object will have properties corresponding to each validation error. For example, if the input is required and empty, there will be a required property. If the input does not meet the minlength, there will be a minlength property.
- dirty: A boolean value indicating whether the control's value has been changed.
- touched: A boolean value indicating whether the control has been blurred (lost focus).

Displaying Error Messages Conditionally:

You can use the *ngIf directive to conditionally display error messages based on the validation state of the form control:

```
    <div>
  <label for="nameInput">Name:</label>
  <input type="text" id="nameInput" [(ngModel)]="name"
name="name" required minlength="3" #nameInput="ngModel">
  <div *ngIf="nameInput.invalid && (nameInput.dirty ||
nameInput.touched)" class="error-message">
    <div *ngIf="nameInput.errors?.required">Name is
required.</div>
    <div *ngIf="nameInput.errors?.minlength">Name must be at
least 3 characters long.</div>
  </div>
</div>
```

Explanation:

- *ngIf="nameInput.invalid && (nameInput.dirty || nameInput.touched)": This *ngIf directive checks if the nameInput is invalid AND if the user has either modified it (dirty) OR blurred the control (touched). This prevents error messages from appearing immediately when the form loads.
- *ngIf="nameInput.errors?.required": Displays the "Name is required." message if the required validator fails.
- *ngIf="nameInput.errors?.minlength": Displays the "Name must be at least 3 characters long." message if the minlength validator fails.

Personal Insight: I've found that providing clear and informative error messages is crucial for improving the user experience. Users are more likely to complete a form successfully if they understand what's wrong and how to fix it.

Beyond HTML5 Attributes: Custom Validation

While HTML5 validation attributes provide a solid foundation for basic form validation, you may need to create your own custom validation logic to handle more complex scenarios. This is where custom validators come into play (more on this in a later section).

A Note on Styling:

It's important to style your validation error messages to make them stand out and easy to see. Use CSS to make the error messages red, bold, or otherwise visually distinctive.

Conclusion: Ensuring High-Quality Input

Form validation is a critical step in building robust and user-friendly web applications. By mastering basic form validation techniques using HTML5 attributes and template variables, you can ensure that your application receives high-quality data, improving the overall user experience and preventing errors. You are now a guardian of data integrity!

8.5 Building a Contact Form: A Symphony of User Interaction

We've explored individual form elements, data binding, and validation. Now, let's bring it all together and build a practical, real-world example: a contact form. Think of this as orchestrating all the form elements you now understand into a coherent and functional user experience, creating a seamless pathway for users to connect with you.

From Individual Elements to a Cohesive Unit: A Practical Application

A contact form is a common feature in many web applications, allowing users to send messages or inquiries to the website owner. Building a contact form provides a great opportunity to apply the concepts we've learned and see how they work together in a real-world scenario.

The Requirements: A Functional and User-Friendly Contact Form

Our contact form will have the following features:

- Input fields for the user's name, email address, and message.
- Validation to ensure that all required fields are filled out and that the email address is valid.
- Clear and informative error messages to guide the user.
- A submit button to send the message.
- Basic styling to make the form visually appealing.
- A confirmation message after successful submission.

Step-by-Step Implementation:

1. **Create a New Component:** Use the Angular CLI to create a new component named contact-form:

```
ng generate component contact-form
```

2. **Define the Component's Properties:** In the contact-form.component.ts file, define the following properties:

```
import { Component } from '@angular/core';

@Component({
  selector: 'app-contact-form',
  templateUrl: './contact-form.component.html',
  styleUrls: ['./contact-form.component.css']
})
export class ContactFormComponent {
  name: string = '';
  email: string = '';
```

147

```
  message: string = '';
  isSubmitted: boolean = false; // Track form submission
status

  onSubmit(): void {
    // Handle form submission logic here (e.g., send data to
a server)
    console.log('Form submitted!');
    console.log('Name:', this.name);
    console.log('Email:', this.email);
    console.log('Message:', this.message);

    this.isSubmitted = true; // Set submission status to true

    // Reset the form after successful submission (optional)
    this.name = '';
    this.email = '';
    this.message = '';
  }
}
```

Explanation:

- name, email, and message: These properties store the values entered by the user in the form.
- isSubmitted: This property tracks whether the form has been submitted.
- onSubmit(): This method handles the form submission logic. It logs the form data to the console and sets the isSubmitted property to true.

3. **Create the HTML Template:** In the contact-form.component.html file, create the HTML template for the form:

```
    <div class="contact-form-container">
  <h2>Contact Us</h2>
  <form (ngSubmit)="onSubmit($event)">
    <div class="form-group">
      <label for="nameInput">Name:</label>
      <input type="text" id="nameInput" [(ngModel)]="name"
name="name" required minlength="3" #nameInput="ngModel"
class="form-control">
      <div *ngIf="nameInput.invalid && (nameInput.dirty ||
nameInput.touched)" class="error-message">
        <div *ngIf="nameInput.errors?.required">Name is
required.</div>
        <div *ngIf="nameInput.errors?.minlength">Name must be
at least 3 characters long.</div>
```

```
        </div>
    </div>

    <div class="form-group">
        <label for="emailInput">Email:</label>
        <input type="email" id="emailInput" [(ngModel)]="email"
name="email" required email #emailInput="ngModel"
class="form-control">
        <div *ngIf="emailInput.invalid && (emailInput.dirty ||
emailInput.touched)" class="error-message">
            <div *ngIf="emailInput.errors?.required">Email is
required.</div>
            <div *ngIf="emailInput.errors?.email">Email must be a
valid email address.</div>
        </div>
    </div>

    <div class="form-group">
        <label for="messageInput">Message:</label>
        <textarea id="messageInput" [(ngModel)]="message"
name="message" required minlength="10" rows="4"
#messageInput="ngModel" class="form-control"></textarea>
        <div *ngIf="messageInput.invalid && (messageInput.dirty
|| messageInput.touched)" class="error-message">
            <div *ngIf="messageInput.errors?.required">Message is
required.</div>
            <div *ngIf="messageInput.errors?.minlength">Message
must be at least 10 characters long.</div>
        </div>
    </div>

    <button type="submit" class="btn btn-primary">Send
Message</button>
  </form>

  <div *ngIf="isSubmitted" class="success-message">
    Thank you for your message! We will get back to you soon.
  </div>
</div>
```

Explanation:

- o <form (ngSubmit)="onSubmit($event)">: This binds the ngSubmit event to the onSubmit() method in the component. The $event is passed to the method, which lets you call event.preventDefault().
- o [(ngModel)]: This directive is used for two-way data binding for each form control.

- required, minlength, email: These HTML5 validation attributes are used to validate the form inputs.
- #nameInput="ngModel", #emailInput="ngModel", #messageInput="ngModel": These template variables provide access to the validation state of each form control.
- *ngIf="nameInput.invalid && (nameInput.dirty || nameInput.touched)": This directive is used to conditionally display error messages based on the validation state of the form controls.
- *ngIf="isSubmitted": This directive displays a success message after the form has been submitted.

4. **Add Styling (Optional):** In the contact-form.component.css file, add some styling to make the form look nice:

```css
.contact-form-container {
max-width: 600px;
margin: 20px auto;
padding: 20px;
border: 1px solid #ccc;
border-radius: 5px;
}

.form-group {
  margin-bottom: 15px;
}

label {
  display: block;
  font-weight: bold;
  margin-bottom: 5px;
}

.form-control {
  width: 100%;
  padding: 8px;
  border: 1px solid #ccc;
  border-radius: 4px;
}

.error-message {
  color: red;
  font-size: 14px;
  margin-top: 5px;
}

.btn-primary {
  background-color: #007bff;
  color: #fff;
```

```
  padding: 10px 20px;
  border: none;
  border-radius: 4px;
  cursor: pointer;
}

.success-message {
  color: green;
  font-weight: bold;
  margin-top: 15px;
}
```

5. **Use the Component in Your Application:** In your
   app.component.html file, add the <app-contact-form> tag to display
   the contact form:

```
  <div style="text-align:center">
<h1>
  Welcome to {{ title }}!
</h1>
  <app-contact-form></app-contact-form>
</div>
```

Putting It All Together

You've now successfully created a contact form that demonstrates:

- Two-way data binding with [(ngModel)].
- HTML5 validation attributes for basic form validation.
- Template variables to check form control validity and display error
  messages.
- Conditional display of a success message after the form has been
  submitted.

Analysis: Deconstructing the Contact Form

- **Data Binding:** [(ngModel)] is used to bind the input fields to the
  corresponding properties in the component, ensuring that the form
  data is automatically synchronized.
- **Validation:** The required, minlength, and email attributes are used to
  enforce basic validation rules, ensuring that the data entered by the
  user is valid.

- **Error Handling:** Template variables and the *ngIf directive are used to conditionally display error messages to the user, providing them with feedback about what they need to fix.
- **Submission Handling:** The (ngSubmit) event binding calls the onSubmit() method when the form is submitted, allowing you to process the form data.

Personal Insight: Building a contact form is a rite of passage for any web developer. It's a great way to put your skills to the test and see how all the pieces of the puzzle fit together.

Beyond the Basics: Enhancing the Contact Form

Here are some ideas for enhancing the contact form:

- Add custom validation to handle more complex validation requirements.
- Implement a more sophisticated error handling mechanism to display server-side validation errors.
- Use a service to send the form data to a backend API.
- Add a CAPTCHA to prevent spam submissions.
- Use a CSS framework (e.g., Bootstrap, Materialize) to improve the styling of the form.

Conclusion: Creating Engaging User Interaction

Building a contact form is a valuable exercise that demonstrates the power and flexibility of Angular's template-driven forms. By mastering the techniques outlined in this section, you can create interactive user interfaces that allow users to input data, submit requests, and connect with your application in meaningful ways. It's the starting point for building more elaborate user interfaces. You are now ready to build interactive experiences!

Chapter 9: Component Communication - Building a Harmonious Ecosystem

We've learned how to create individual components, but the real power of Angular comes from composing these components to create complex and interactive applications. Component communication is the key to making your components work together, allowing them to share data, respond to events, and create a seamless user experience. Think of component communication as establishing clear channels between different parts of your application, ensuring that information flows smoothly and efficiently.

Why is Component Communication Important?

Component communication enables you to:

- **Create Modular Applications:** Break down your application into smaller, self-contained units that are easier to develop, test, and maintain.
- **Share Data Effectively:** Pass data between components without tightly coupling them.
- **Handle User Interactions:** Allow child components to notify parent components of user actions (e.g., button clicks, form submissions).
- **Create Reusable Components:** Build components that can be used in different parts of your application, adapting their behavior based on the data they receive.

9.1 @Input(): Passing Data to Child Components- The One-Way Flow of Information

We're diving into the crucial realm of component communication, and @Input() is our starting point. Think of @Input() as establishing a clear, one-way channel for information to flow from a parent component *down* to a child component. It's how you equip child components with the data they need to render and function correctly.

Beyond Isolated Pieces: Connecting the Building Blocks

While individual components form the structure of your Angular application, they rarely operate in complete isolation. They often need data from other components to display information, react to user actions, or perform specific tasks. @Input() provides a structured and controlled way to share this data.

The Mechanics of @Input(): Exposing Properties for Parent Access

@Input() works by decorating a property in the child component with the @Input() decorator from @angular/core. This signals to Angular that this property is intended to receive data from the parent component. When the parent component uses the child component in its template, it can bind to this input property using property binding (square brackets []).

Syntax: Decorating and Binding

1. **Child Component:**

```
     // child.component.ts
import { Component, Input } from '@angular/core';

@Component({
  selector: 'app-child',
  templateUrl: './child.component.html',
  styleUrls: ['./child.component.css']
})
export class ChildComponent {
  @Input() message: string = ''; // The input property
}
```

2. **Parent Component Template:**

```
     <!-- parent.component.html -->
<app-child [message]="parentData"></app-child>
```

Key Components Explained:

- @Input(): The decorator that marks the message property in the ChildComponent as an input. This makes it available for binding in the parent's template.
- message: string = ": Defines the input property. While not strictly required, providing a default value helps prevent errors if the parent doesn't provide a value and makes your component more robust.
- <app-child>: The tag that represents the child component in the parent's template.

- [message]="parentData": The property binding syntax that connects the message input property of the ChildComponent to the parentData property of the ParentComponent. The square brackets [] indicate property binding.

Passing Different Data Types:

You can pass data of any type to a child component using @Input(), including:

- Strings
- Numbers
- Booleans
- Arrays
- Objects
- Functions (though this is less common and should be used carefully)

Example: Passing Product Data to a Product Card Component

Let's say you're building an e-commerce application and you want to display product information in a reusable card component. You can use @Input() to pass the product data from a parent component to the ProductCardComponent.

1. **Product Card Component:**

```typescript
// product-card.component.ts
import { Component, Input } from '@angular/core';

@Component({
  selector: 'app-product-card',
  templateUrl: './product-card.component.html',
  styleUrls: ['./product-card.component.css']
})
export class ProductCardComponent {
  @Input() product: any; // Input property for product data
}
```

2. **Product Card Template:**

```html
<!-- product-card.component.html -->
<div class="product-card">
  <h2>{{ product.name }}</h2>
  <img [src]="product.imageUrl" alt="{{ product.name }}">
```

```
  <p>{{ product.description }}</p>
  <p>Price: ${{ product.price }}</p>
</div>
```

3. **Parent Component:**

```
    // product-list.component.ts
import { Component } from '@angular/core';

@Component({
  selector: 'app-product-list',
  templateUrl: './product-list.component.html',
  styleUrls: ['./product-list.component.css']
})
export class ProductListComponent {
  products = [
    { name: 'Awesome Product', description: 'This is an
awesome product.', price: 99.99, imageUrl:
'https://via.placeholder.com/150' },
    { name: 'Another Product', description: 'This is another
product.', price: 49.99, imageUrl:
'https://via.placeholder.com/150' }
  ];
}
```

4. **Parent Component Template:**

```
    <!-- product-list.component.html -->
<h1>Product List</h1>
<div *ngFor="let product of products">
  <app-product-card [product]="product"></app-product-card>
</div>
```

Personal Insight: I use @Input() constantly to create reusable components. It allows me to build components that can be easily configured and adapted to different parts of my application.

A Note on Data Mutation: Be Mindful of Immutability

It's *extremely important* to avoid directly modifying the input data in your child component. If you do so, you'll inadvertently change the data in the parent component as well, leading to unexpected behavior and difficult-to-debug issues.

If you need to modify the data, create a *copy* of the data in the child component and modify the copy instead.

Here's why this is crucial:

- **Referential Equality:** In JavaScript, objects and arrays are passed by reference. This means that when you pass an object or array to a function (or a component), you're actually passing a *reference* to the original object or array. If the function modifies the object or array, it's actually modifying the original object or array, not a copy.
- **One-Way Data Flow:** Angular encourages a one-way data flow, where data flows from the parent component to the child component. This makes it easier to reason about your application's state and prevent unexpected side effects. Modifying input data in the child component violates this principle.

Conclusion: Passing Data Down the Component Tree

@Input() is a fundamental tool for passing data from parent components to child components in Angular. By mastering @Input(), you can create reusable, configurable, and well-structured applications that are easy to develop, test, and maintain. You are now a master of the one-way data flow!

9.2 @Output(): Emitting Events from Child Components- Signaling Action Upwards

We've learned how @Input() lets parents pass data *down* to their children. But what about the other direction? What if a child component needs to notify its parent that something important has happened, such as a button click, a form submission, or a change in its internal state? This is where @Output() comes in. Think of @Output() as establishing a clear channel for events to flow *upwards* from a child component to its parent.

Beyond Data Reception: Empowering Children to Communicate

While children often passively display data passed from their parents, they are also capable of initiating actions and managing their own internal state. @Output() provides a mechanism for children to communicate these actions and state changes to their parents, allowing the parent components to respond accordingly.

The Mechanics of @Output(): Broadcasting Events Up the Tree

@Output() works by creating a custom event emitter in the child component. The child component can then trigger this event emitter to notify the parent component that something has happened. The parent component listens for this event and executes a corresponding handler function.

The Syntax: Decorating and Reacting

1. **Child Component:**

```
// child.component.ts
import { Component, Output, EventEmitter } from
'@angular/core';

@Component({
  selector: 'app-child',
  templateUrl: './child.component.html',
  styleUrls: ['./child.component.css']
})
export class ChildComponent {
  @Output() itemClicked = new EventEmitter<number>(); //
Output property
}
```

2. **Parent Component Template:**

```
<!-- parent.component.html -->
<app-child (itemClicked)="handleItemClick($event)"></app-
child>
```

Key Components Explained:

- @Output(): The decorator that marks the itemClicked property in the ChildComponent as an output. This makes it available for binding in the parent's template.
- itemClicked = new EventEmitter<number>(): Defines the output property as an EventEmitter. The <number> specifies the type of data that will be emitted with the event.
- <app-child>: The tag that represents the child component in the parent's template.

- (itemClicked)="handleItemClick($event)": The event binding syntax that listens for the itemClicked output from the ChildComponent and calls the handleItemClick() method in the ParentComponent.
- $event: The data emitted by the child component when the event is triggered.

Example: Emitting a Product ID to the Parent Component

Let's revisit our product card example. Suppose we want to notify the parent component when the user clicks a "View Details" button in the ProductCardComponent. We can use @Output() to emit the product ID to the parent.

1. **Product Card Component:**

```typescript
// product-card.component.ts
import { Component, Input, Output, EventEmitter } from
'@angular/core';

@Component({
  selector: 'app-product-card',
  templateUrl: './product-card.component.html',
  styleUrls: ['./product-card.component.css']
})
export class ProductCardComponent {
  @Input() product: any;
  @Output() viewDetailsClicked = new EventEmitter<number>();
// Output event

  onViewDetailsClick(): void {
    this.viewDetailsClicked.emit(this.product.id); // Emit
the product ID
  }
}
```

2. **Product Card Template:**

```html
<!-- product-card.component.html -->
<div class="product-card">
  <h2>{{ product.name }}</h2>
  <img [src]="product.imageUrl" alt="{{ product.name }}">
  <p>{{ product.description }}</p>
  <p>Price: ${{ product.price }}</p>
  <button (click)="onViewDetailsClick()">View
Details</button>
</div>
```

3. Product List Component:

```typescript
// product-list.component.ts
import { Component } from '@angular/core';

@Component({
  selector: 'app-product-list',
  templateUrl: './product-list.component.html',
  styleUrls: ['./product-list.component.css']
})
export class ProductListComponent {
  products = [
    { id: 1, name: 'Awesome Product', description: 'This is
an awesome product.', price: 99.99, imageUrl:
'https://via.placeholder.com/150' },
    { id: 2, name: 'Another Product', description: 'This is
another product.', price: 49.99, imageUrl:
'https://via.placeholder.com/150' }
  ];

  handleViewDetails(productId: number): void {
    alert(`View details clicked for product ID:
${productId}`);
  }
}
```

4. Product List Template:

```html
<!-- product-list.component.html -->
<h1>Product List</h1>
<div *ngFor="let product of products">
  <app-product-card [product]="product"
(viewDetailsClicked)="handleViewDetails($event)"></app-
product-card>
</div>
```

Understanding the EventEmitter:

The EventEmitter class is a special class in Angular that allows you to emit events. It is actually a subclass of RxJS's Subject, which means it's an observable that can emit values over time.

Key Points About EventEmitter:

- **emit(value):** This method is used to emit an event with a specified value. The value can be of any data type.
- **subscribe(callback):** The parent component uses event binding ((event)="handler($event)") to effectively subscribe to the event emitted by the EventEmitter.

Personal Insight: @Output() and EventEmitter are essential for creating interactive components that respond to user actions and communicate with their parent components. It enables a robust pattern of communication between components in an Angular application.

A Note on Naming Conventions:

It's best practice to name your output properties using the Event suffix (e.g., itemClicked, formSubmitted, valueChanged). This makes it clear that the property is an output and that it emits events.

Conclusion: Sending Signals Up the Component Tree

@Output() and EventEmitter are fundamental tools for enabling child components to communicate with their parent components in Angular. By mastering these techniques, you can build applications that are both modular and responsive, creating a seamless and engaging user experience. You have now mastered the art of upward communication, empowering your child components to signal important events to their parents. You are now a master communicator!

9.3 Building a Reusable Card Component: A Symphony of Communication and Design

We've explored @Input() for data flowing down and @Output() for events flowing up. Now, let's solidify our understanding of component communication by building a practical, real-world example: a reusable card component. Think of this as creating a versatile building block that can be used to display information about a variety of different types of content, showcasing the true power of componentization.

Beyond Simple Display: A Versatile UI Element

A card component is a common UI pattern that is used to display information in a visually appealing and organized way. It typically includes a title, image, description, and action buttons. Building a reusable card component allows you to easily display different types of content (e.g., products, articles, profiles) in a consistent and visually appealing format throughout your application.

The Requirements: A Flexible and Customizable Card

Our reusable card component will have the following features:

- @Input() properties for the card's title, description, and image URL, allowing the parent component to customize the content of the card.
- An @Output() property for a button click event, allowing the parent component to respond when the user clicks a button in the card.
- Basic styling to make the card visually appealing.
- Flexibility to adapt to different content types.

Step-by-Step Implementation:

1. **Create a New Component:** Use the Angular CLI to create a new component named card:

```
ng generate component card
```

2. **Define the Component's Properties:** In the card.component.ts file, define the following properties:

```
import { Component, Input, Output, EventEmitter } from '@angular/core';

@Component({
  selector: 'app-card',
  templateUrl: './card.component.html',
  styleUrls: ['./card.component.css']
})
export class CardComponent {
  @Input() title: string = '';
  @Input() description: string = '';
  @Input() imageUrl: string = '';
  @Input() buttonText: string = 'Learn More'; // Add a configurable button text
  @Output() buttonClick = new EventEmitter<string>();

  onButtonClick(): void {
    this.buttonClick.emit(this.title); // Emit the title as event data
```

```
        }
    }
}
```

Explanation:

- @Input() title: string = '': An input property for the card's title. It has a default value of an empty string.
- @Input() description: string = '': An input property for the card's description. It has a default value of an empty string.
- @Input() imageUrl: string = '': An input property for the card's image URL. It has a default value of an empty string.
- @Input() buttonText: string = 'Learn More': An input property for the button's text. It has a default value of "Learn More." This adds even more customization.
- @Output() buttonClick = new EventEmitter<string>(): An output property for the button click event. It emits the card's title as event data.
- onButtonClick(): This method is called when the button is clicked. It emits the buttonClick event, passing the card's title as the event data.

3. **Create the HTML Template:** In the card.component.html file, create the HTML template for the component:

```
    <div class="card">
    <img [src]="imageUrl" alt="Card Image">
    <h2>{{ title }}</h2>
    <p>{{ description }}</p>
    <button (click)="onButtonClick()">{{ buttonText }}</button>
</div>
```

Explanation:

- <img [src]="imageUrl" alt="Card Image">: Displays the card's image using property binding.
- <h2>{{ title }}</h2>: Displays the card's title using interpolation.
- <p>{{ description }}</p>: Displays the card's description using interpolation.
- <button (click)="onButtonClick()">{{ buttonText }}</button>: Displays a button that calls the onButtonClick() method when clicked and displays the button text using interpolation.

4. **Add Styling (Optional):** In the card.component.css file, add some styling to make the card look nice:

```css
    .card {
  border: 1px solid #ccc;
  padding: 10px;
  margin: 10px;
  text-align: center;
}

.card img {
  width: 100%;
  max-height: 150px;
  object-fit: cover;
}
```

5. **Use the Component in Your Application:** In your parent component (e.g., app.component.ts), define the data for the card:

```typescript
    // app.component.ts
import { Component } from '@angular/core';

@Component({
  selector: 'app-root',
  templateUrl: './app.component.html',
  styleUrls: ['./app.component.css']
})
export class AppComponent {
  cardTitle: string = 'Awesome Product';
  cardDescription: string = 'This is a description of the
awesome product.';
  cardImageUrl: string = 'https://via.placeholder.com/150';

  handleButtonClick(title: string): void {
    alert(`Button clicked for: ${title}`);
  }
}
```

6. **Add the Card Component to the Parent Component's Template:** In the app.component.html file, add the <app-card> tag to display the card:

```html
    <div style="text-align:center">
  <h1>
    Welcome to {{ title }}!
  </h1>
```

```
  <app-card [title]="cardTitle"
[description]="cardDescription" [imageUrl]="cardImageUrl"
[buttonText]="'View More'"
(buttonClick)="handleButtonClick($event)"></app-card>
</div>
```

Analysis: Decoding the Reusable Card Component

- @Input() Properties: The title, description, and imageUrl properties are decorated with @Input(), allowing the parent component to customize the content of the card.
- @Output() Property: The buttonClick property is decorated with @Output(), allowing the parent component to respond when the user clicks the button in the card.
- onButtonClick() Method: This method is called when the button is clicked. It emits the buttonClick event, passing the card's title as the event data.
- Property Binding and Event Binding: The parent component uses property binding to pass data to the card and event binding to listen for the buttonClick event.

Flexibility and Reusability: The Power of This Pattern

The beauty of this component lies in its reusability. Because the data is passed in and the action button is signaled upward, *any* component can use this card. You can create a list of articles, people, or services, and this same card will work for all. You just need to pass in the right parameters.

Personal Insight: Building reusable components is one of the most important skills you can develop as an Angular developer. It allows you to create applications that are easy to maintain, test, and scale.

Beyond the Basics: Enhancing the Card Component

Here are some ideas for enhancing the card component:

- Add support for different card layouts (e.g., a card with a left-aligned image, a card with a full-width image).
- Add support for different button styles (e.g., a primary button, a secondary button, a link button).
- Add support for displaying additional information in the card, such as a rating, a price, or a date.

- Allow the parent component to pass in a custom template for the card's content.

Conclusion: Building Reusable UI Elements

Building a reusable card component demonstrates how you can use @Input() and @Output() to create flexible and configurable components in Angular. By mastering these techniques, you can build applications that are easy to maintain, test, and scale. You now have the skills to create reusable UI elements that can be used throughout your applications, saving you time and effort and ensuring a consistent user experience! You are now a component architect!

Chapter 10: Project: Build a To-Do List App - A Practical Synthesis of Angular Skills

We've covered a lot of ground so far, exploring core Angular concepts and techniques. Now it's time to put everything into practice and build a complete application from scratch: a classic to-do list app. Think of this as conducting your own orchestra, bringing together all the instruments (components, directives, pipes, services) to create a beautiful and functional symphony of code.

Why a To-Do List? A Versatile Learning Platform

A to-do list app is a simple yet powerful project that allows you to demonstrate a wide range of Angular skills:

- **Component Creation and Communication:** Structuring the application into reusable components.
- **Data Binding:** Displaying and updating data using interpolation, property binding, event binding, and two-way binding.
- **Directives:** Conditionally rendering elements and iterating over data using *ngIf and *ngFor.
- **Services and Dependency Injection:** Creating and injecting services to manage data and logic.
- **User Input and Forms:** Gathering user input and validating it using forms.
- **Styling:** Applying CSS to create a visually appealing user interface.

10.1 Project Requirements: Charting the Course for Our To-Do List App

Before we write a single line of code, it's crucial to define exactly *what* our to-do list application should do. This is where the magic happens: meticulously defining the project requirements. Think of this as creating a blueprint before building a house – it provides a clear roadmap and prevents us from wandering aimlessly.

Beyond Wishful Thinking: The Importance of Clear Requirements

Clearly defined requirements are the bedrock of any successful software project. They:

- **Provide Clarity:** They establish a shared understanding of what the application should do.
- **Guide Development:** They provide a roadmap for developers to follow, ensuring that they build the right features.
- **Enable Testing:** They provide a basis for testing the application and verifying that it meets the desired functionality.
- **Manage Scope:** They help to prevent scope creep by clearly defining what is and is not included in the project.

Defining Functional and Non-Functional Requirements

Project requirements typically fall into two categories:

- **Functional Requirements:** These describe *what* the application should do. They specify the features and functionalities that the application must provide. Functional Requirements are things the application *does*.
- **Non-Functional Requirements:** These describe *how* the application should behave. They specify the qualities of the application, such as its performance, security, usability, and maintainability. Non-Functional Requirements are qualities the application *has*.

For our simple to-do list app, we'll focus primarily on functional requirements, but it's important to be aware of non-functional requirements as well.

Functional Requirements: The To-Do List App's Core Features

Let's define the functional requirements for our to-do list app. These are the core actions that the application should allow the user to perform:

- **Add Tasks:**
  - The user should be able to add new tasks to the list.
  - Each task should have a description.
  - The user should be able to enter the description in a text input field.
  - Pressing the "Add Task" button should add the task to the list.
- **View Tasks:**
  - The user should be able to see a list of all tasks.

- Each task should display its description and its completion status.
- **Mark Tasks as Complete:**
  - The user should be able to mark tasks as complete.
  - Each task should have a checkbox that the user can click to toggle its completion status.
  - When a task is marked as complete, its appearance should change to indicate its completion status (e.g., by striking through the text).
- **Delete Tasks:**
  - The user should be able to delete tasks from the list.
  - Each task should have a "Delete" button that the user can click to remove it from the list.
- **Persistence:**
  - The list of tasks should be persisted across sessions. This means that when the user closes the browser and reopens the application, the list of tasks should be preserved.
  - We'll use local storage to persist the data.
- **Clear Completed Tasks:**
  - The user should be able to delete all completed tasks from the list with a single click.
  - There should be a "Clear Completed" button that the user can click to remove all completed tasks from the list.

UI Requirements: Designing a User-Friendly Interface

Now, let's define the UI requirements for our to-do list app. These requirements specify how the application should look and feel. These determine what the user will *see*:

- **Task Input Form:**
  - A text input field for entering new tasks.
  - An "Add Task" button to add the task to the list.
- **Task List:**
  - A list of tasks, with each task displayed as a list item.
  - Each list item should display the task's description and a checkbox to mark it as complete.
  - Each list item should have a "Delete" button.
- **Clear Completed Button:**
  - A "Clear Completed" button to remove all completed tasks from the list.
- **Labels and Instructions:**

- o Clear and informative labels and instructions to guide the user.
- **Styling:**
  - o Visually appealing styling that is consistent with the rest of the application.

Non-Functional Requirements: A Glimpse Beyond the Surface (Mostly Implicit in This Example)

While we're primarily focusing on functional requirements, it's important to acknowledge the non-functional requirements that will also influence our design decisions, even if we don't explicitly address them:

- **Usability:** The application should be easy to use and understand.
- **Performance:** The application should be responsive and performant.
- **Accessibility:** The application should be accessible to users with disabilities.
- **Maintainability:** The code should be well-organized and easy to maintain.

Personal Insight: I've learned the hard way that spending time upfront to define clear requirements can save you a lot of time and frustration later on. It's an investment that always pays off.

A Note on Scope Creep:

Scope creep is the tendency for projects to gradually expand beyond their original scope. This can lead to delays, cost overruns, and ultimately, project failure. It's important to manage scope creep by carefully controlling changes to the project requirements and making sure that any new features are justified and aligned with the project goals.

Conclusion: A Solid Foundation for Success

Defining clear and concise requirements is a critical first step in building any software project. By taking the time to understand the functional and UI requirements for our to-do list app, we've laid a solid foundation for success. We now have a clear roadmap to guide our development efforts and ensure that we build an application that meets the needs of our users. It's time to start building!

10.2 Component and Service Structure: Building a Solid Architectural Foundation

Now that we have a firm grasp on the requirements, the next crucial step is to plan the architecture of our to-do list application. Think of this as designing the internal framework of a building – ensuring that all the components are well-connected, easily accessible, and contribute to a stable and functional structure. This step will dictate how we organize our code, how different parts of the application interact, and how easy it will be to maintain and scale our application in the future.

Beyond Code Organization: The Importance of Architectural Decisions

Choosing the right component and service structure is not just about organizing files and folders; it's about making fundamental design decisions that will impact the entire application. A well-designed architecture can:

- **Improve Code Maintainability:** Make it easier to understand, modify, and debug your code.
- **Enhance Code Reusability:** Enable you to reuse components and services in different parts of your application.
- **Increase Testability:** Make it easier to write unit tests and integration tests for your application.
- **Promote Scalability:** Allow your application to grow and evolve over time without becoming a tangled mess.
- **Facilitate Collaboration:** Make it easier for multiple developers to work on the same application.

The Key Architectural Elements: Components and Services

In Angular, the two primary building blocks for structuring applications are components and services:

- **Components:** As we know, components are self-contained UI elements that encapsulate the logic, template, and styling for a specific part of the user interface. They are responsible for rendering a specific view and handling user interactions within that view.
- **Services:** Services are classes that encapsulate reusable logic and data access. They are typically used to perform tasks that are not specific to any particular component, such as fetching data from a server, managing application state, or providing utility functions.

171

The Architectural Blueprint: Our To-Do List App's Structure

Based on the project requirements, we can break down our to-do list app into the following components and services:

Components:

- **TodoListComponent:**
  - **Responsibility:** This component will be the main container for the to-do list. It will be responsible for:
    - Displaying the list of tasks.
    - Providing a form for adding new tasks.
    - Handling the completion and deletion of tasks.
    - Providing a button to clear all completed tasks.
  - **Dependencies:** It will depend on the TodoService to manage the list of tasks.
- **TodoItemComponent:**
  - **Responsibility:** This component will represent a single to-do list item. It will be responsible for:
    - Displaying the task's description.
    - Providing a checkbox to mark the task as complete.
    - Providing a button to delete the task.
  - **Dependencies:** It will not have any dependencies on other components or services. It will simply receive data from its parent component (TodoListComponent) and emit events when the user interacts with it.

Services:

- **TodoService:**
  - **Responsibility:** This service will be responsible for managing the list of tasks. It will provide methods for:
    - Adding tasks.
    - Deleting tasks.
    - Marking tasks as complete.
    - Retrieving the list of tasks from local storage.
    - Saving the list of tasks to local storage.
    - Clearing all completed tasks.
  - **Dependencies:** It will not have any dependencies on other components or services. It will operate independently, managing the data for the entire application.

Component Hierarchy: A Visual Representation

To better understand the relationship between the components, we can represent them in a hierarchy:

```
    AppComponent (The overall application)
 └── TodoListComponent (The container for the to-do list)
     └── TodoItemComponent (repeated for each task)
(Represents an individual to-do item)
```

This hierarchy shows that the TodoListComponent is a child of the AppComponent, and the TodoItemComponent is a child of the TodoListComponent. This hierarchy will guide how we pass data and events between the components.

Justification for Our Architectural Choices

- **Separation of Concerns:** We've separated the UI logic from the data management logic. The components are responsible for rendering the UI and handling user interactions, while the service is responsible for managing the data. This makes the code more modular, testable, and maintainable.
- **Reusability:** The TodoItemComponent is designed to be reusable. It can be used to display any to-do list item, regardless of its content or status.
- **Testability:** Each component and service can be tested independently, making it easier to ensure the quality of our code.
- **Scalability:** The architecture is designed to be scalable. If we need to add new features or functionalities to the to-do list app, we can do so without making significant changes to the existing code.

Alternative Architectures: Considering Other Options (Briefly)

While our chosen architecture is well-suited for this simple application, it's important to acknowledge that there are other architectural options that we could have considered:

- **Using a State Management Library (e.g., NgRx, Akita):** For more complex applications, a state management library can provide a more structured and predictable way to manage application state. However, for our simple to-do list app, a state management library would be overkill.

173

- **Using a Backend API:** For more sophisticated applications, you might want to store the to-do list data in a backend database and use a backend API to manage the data. However, for our simple example, we'll use local storage to keep things simple.

Personal Insight: I've found that spending time upfront to plan the architecture of your application can save you a lot of time and effort in the long run. It's an investment that pays off in terms of code quality, maintainability, and scalability.

Conclusion: A Blueprint for Success

By carefully planning the component and service structure of our to-do list app, we've laid a solid foundation for success. We now have a clear understanding of the responsibilities of each component and service, and we're ready to start implementing the UI and functionality of our application. It's time to build!

10.3 Implementing the UI: Weaving the Visual Tapestry of Our Application

With our architecture in place, it's time to breathe life into our to-do list app by implementing the user interface. Think of this as the artistic phase of the project, carefully arranging the visual elements to create an engaging and intuitive experience for the user.

Beyond Wireframes: Translating Design into Code

Implementing the UI is more than just translating wireframes or mockups into HTML and CSS. It's about understanding the user's needs and creating an interface that is both functional and visually appealing. It involves making decisions about layout, typography, color, and interaction design.

The Key Ingredients: HTML, CSS, and Angular Directives

We'll be using the following technologies to implement the UI:

- **HTML:** To define the structure of the user interface.
- **CSS:** To style the user interface and make it visually appealing.
- **Angular Directives:** To add dynamic behavior to the user interface, such as conditionally rendering elements and iterating over data.

Step-by-Step Implementation: Building the UI Elements

1. **Implement the TodoItcmComponent Template:** This component represents a single to-do list item. Let's focus on visually representing the completion status and action items.

```
<li [class.completed]="task.isCompleted">
  <input type="checkbox" [checked]="task.isCompleted"
(change)="onComplete()">
  <span>{{ task.description }}</span>
  <button (click)="onDelete()">Delete</button>
</li>
```

   Explanation:

   o [class.completed]="task.isCompleted": This uses property binding to dynamically add the completed class to the list item if the task.isCompleted property is true. We'll define the styling for the completed class in the CSS file.
   o <input type="checkbox" [checked]="task.isCompleted" (change)="onComplete()">: This displays a checkbox that is checked if the task

10.4 Adding Functionality: Breathing Life into Our Application

With the UI elements in place, it's time to wire them up to our TodoService and make our to-do list app truly interactive. Think of this as installing the plumbing and electrical systems in our house, making sure everything connects properly and functions as intended. This is where our application starts to actually *do* things.

Beyond Static Markup: Making the UI Respond to User Input

Adding functionality involves connecting the UI elements to the component's logic and data, allowing the application to respond to user interactions such as adding, deleting, and completing tasks. This is where we'll be using data binding, event binding, and dependency injection to bring our to-do list app to life.

The Key Actions: Connecting Events to Data Manipulation

We'll implement the following actions in our TodoListComponent:

- **Adding Tasks:** Handling the submission of the new task form and adding the task to the list.
- **Deleting Tasks:** Removing a task from the list when the user clicks the "Delete" button.
- **Completing Tasks:** Toggling the completion status of a task when the user clicks the checkbox.
- **Clearing Completed Tasks:** Removing all completed tasks from the list when the user clicks the "Clear Completed" button.

Step-by-Step Implementation: Wiring Up the Functionality

1. **Adding Tasks:**
   - **Connect the Input Field:** In the todo-list.component.html file, we already have the input field bound to the newTaskDescription property using [(ngModel)]:

```
<input type="text" placeholder="Add a new task"
[(ngModel)]="newTaskDescription">
```

   - **Connect the Add Task Button:** In the todo-list.component.html file, we'll connect the "Add Task" button to the addTask() method in the TodoListComponent class using event binding:

```
<button (click)="addTask()">Add Task</button>
```

   - **Implement the addTask() Method:** In the todo-list.component.ts file, implement the addTask() method to add a new task to the list using the TodoService:

```
import { Component, OnInit } from '@angular/core';
import { TodoService } from './todo.service';

@Component({
  selector: 'app-todo-list',
  templateUrl: './todo-list.component.html',
  styleUrls: ['./todo-list.component.css']
})
```

```
export class TodoListComponent implements OnInit {
  tasks: { description: string; isCompleted: boolean }[] =
[];
  newTaskDescription: string = '';

  constructor(private todoService: TodoService) { }

  ngOnInit(): void {
    this.tasks = this.todoService.getTasks();
  }

  addTask(): void {
    if (this.newTaskDescription.trim() !== '') { // Prevent
empty tasks
      this.todoService.addTask(this.newTaskDescription);
      this.newTaskDescription = ''; // Clear the input field
      this.tasks = this.todoService.getTasks(); // Refresh
the task list
    }
  }

  // ... other methods
}
```

2. **Explanation:**
   o if (this.newTaskDescription.trim() !== "): This checks if the input field is not empty after removing leading and trailing whitespace. This prevents the user from adding empty tasks.
   o this.todoService.addTask(this.newTaskDescription): This calls the addTask() method in the TodoService to add the new task to the list.
   o this.newTaskDescription = ";: This clears the input field after the task has been added.
   o this.tasks = this.todoService.getTasks(): This refreshes the task list to reflect the changes. This step is *crucial* for updating the UI.
3. **Deleting Tasks:**
   o **Connect the Delete Button:** In the todo-item.component.html file, we'll connect the "Delete" button to the onDelete() method in the TodoItemComponent class using event binding:

   ```
   <button (click)="onDelete()">Delete</button>
   ```

- o **Implement the onDelete() Method:** In the todo-item.component.ts file, implement the onDelete() method to emit the delete event with the task's index:

```
import { Component, Input, Output, EventEmitter } from '@angular/core';

@Component({
  selector: 'app-todo-item',
  templateUrl: './todo-item.component.html',
  styleUrls: ['./todo-item.component.css']
})
export class TodoItemComponent {
  @Input() task: any;
  @Input() index: number = 0;
  @Output() complete = new EventEmitter<number>();
  @Output() delete = new EventEmitter<number>();

  onComplete(): void {
    this.complete.emit(this.index);
  }

  onDelete(): void {
    this.delete.emit(this.index);
  }
}
```

- o **Handle the delete Event in the TodoListComponent:** In the todo-list.component.ts file, implement the deleteTask() method to handle the delete event emitted by the TodoItemComponent:

```
import { Component, OnInit } from '@angular/core';
import { TodoService } from './todo.service';

@Component({
  selector: 'app-todo-list',
  templateUrl: './todo-list.component.html',
  styleUrls: ['./todo-list.component.css']
})
export class TodoListComponent implements OnInit {
  tasks: { description: string; isCompleted: boolean }[] =
[];
  newTaskDescription: string = '';

  constructor(private todoService: TodoService) { }

  ngOnInit(): void {
```

```
    this.tasks = this.todoService.getTasks();
  }

  // ... other methods

  deleteTask(index: number): void {
    this.todoService.deleteTask(index);
    this.tasks = this.todoService.getTasks(); // Refresh the
task list
  }
}
```

- o **Connect to the Parent:** Make sure the Parent has this in the HTML

```
    <app-todo-item *ngFor="let task of tasks; let i =
index"
            [task]="task" [index]="i"
            (complete)="completeTask($event)"
            (delete)="deleteTask($event)"></app-todo-item>
```

4. **Explanation:**
   - o this.todoService.deleteTask(index): This calls the deleteTask() method in the TodoService to delete the task from the list.
   - o this.tasks = this.todoService.getTasks(): This refreshes the task list to reflect the changes.
5. **Completing Tasks:**
   - o **Connect the Checkbox:** In the todo-item.component.html file, we'll connect the checkbox to the onComplete() method in the TodoItemComponent class using event binding:

```
    <input type="checkbox" [checked]="task.isCompleted"
(change)="onComplete()">
```

   - o **Implement the onComplete() Method:** In the todo-item.component.ts file, implement the onComplete() method to emit the complete event with the task's index: (Already implemented in above step)
   - o **Handle the complete Event in the TodoListComponent:** In the todo-list.component.ts file, implement the completeTask() method to handle the complete event emitted by the TodoItemComponent:

179

```
      import { Component, OnInit } from '@angular/core';
import { TodoService } from './todo.service';

@Component({
  selector: 'app-todo-list',
  templateUrl: './todo-list.component.html',
  styleUrls: ['./todo-list.component.css']
})
export class TodoListComponent implements OnInit {
  tasks: { description: string; isCompleted: boolean }[] =
[];
  newTaskDescription: string = '';

  constructor(private todoService: TodoService) { }

  ngOnInit(): void {
    this.tasks = this.todoService.getTasks();
  }

  // ... other methods

  completeTask(index: number): void {
    this.todoService.completeTask(index);
    this.tasks = this.todoService.getTasks(); // Refresh the
task list
  }
}
```

- o **Connect to the Parent:** Make sure the Parent has this in the HTML

```
      <app-todo-item *ngFor="let task of tasks; let i =
index"
            [task]="task" [index]="i"
            (complete)="completeTask($event)"
            (delete)="deleteTask($event)"></app-todo-item>
```

6. **Explanation:**
   - o this.todoService.completeTask(index): This calls the completeTask() method in the TodoService to toggle the completion status of the task.
   - o this.tasks = this.todoService.getTasks(): This refreshes the task list to reflect the changes.
7. **Clearing Completed Tasks:**
   - o **Connect the Clear Completed Button:** In the todo-list.component.html file, we'll connect the "Clear Completed"

button to the clearCompleted() method in the TodoListComponent class using event binding:

```
<button (click)="clearCompleted()">Clear
Completed</button>
```

- o **Implement the clearCompleted() Method:** In the todo-list.component.ts file, implement the clearCompleted() method to clear all completed tasks using the TodoService:

```
import { Component, OnInit } from '@angular/core';
import { TodoService } from './todo.service';

@Component({
  selector: 'app-todo-list',
  templateUrl: './todo-list.component.html',
  styleUrls: ['./todo-list.component.css']
})
export class TodoListComponent implements OnInit {
  tasks: { description: string; isCompleted: boolean }[] =
[];
  newTaskDescription: string = '';

  constructor(private todoService: TodoService) { }

  ngOnInit(): void {
    this.tasks = this.todoService.getTasks();
  }

  // ... other methods

  clearCompleted(): void {
    this.todoService.clearCompleted();
    this.tasks = this.todoService.getTasks(); // Refresh the
task list
  }
}
```

8. **Explanation:**
   - o this.todoService.clearCompleted(): This calls the clearCompleted() method in the TodoService to clear all completed tasks from the list.
   - o this.tasks = this.todoService.getTasks(): This refreshes the task list to reflect the changes.

Personal Insight: I've found that breaking down complex functionality into smaller, manageable methods makes the code easier to understand, test, and maintain.

A Note on State Management

While this example uses a simple approach to state management (reloading the entire task list after each change), more complex applications may require a more sophisticated state management solution, such as RxJS or NgRx.

Conclusion: Interactivity Unlocked!

By connecting our UI elements to our TodoService, we've brought our to-do list app to life. The user can now add, delete, and complete tasks, and the UI will automatically update to reflect the changes. We now have a truly interactive application.

10.5 Styling the App: Adding the Final Touches of Elegance and Clarity

With the core functionality in place, it's time to focus on the visual presentation of our to-do list app. Think of this as adding the interior design to our house, making it not only functional but also a pleasant and inviting space to be in. Effective styling can significantly enhance the user experience, making the application more intuitive, engaging, and enjoyable to use.

Beyond Functionality: Enhancing Usability and Aesthetics

Styling is not just about making your application look pretty; it's also about improving its usability. A well-styled application is easier to understand, navigate, and use. Clear typography, consistent spacing, and intuitive visual cues can all contribute to a better user experience.

The Tools of the Trade: CSS and Component-Specific Styles

We'll be using CSS to style our to-do list app. In Angular, each component has its own CSS file, allowing you to encapsulate the styling for that component and prevent style conflicts with other parts of the application. This promotes modularity and maintainability.

A Step-by-Step Styling Guide:

We'll focus on styling the key elements of our to-do list app:

1. **Styling the TodoListComponent:**
   - **Container:** We'll add styling to the todo-list-container class to provide a clean and organized layout.
   - **Add Task Form:** We'll style the input field and button to make them visually appealing and easy to use.
   - **Task List:** We'll style the unordered list (<ul>) to remove the default bullet points and add spacing between the list items.
   - **Clear Completed Button:** We'll style the "Clear Completed" button to make it stand out.

```css
/* todo-list.component.css */
.todo-list-container {
  max-width: 600px;
  margin: 20px auto;
  padding: 20px;
  border: 1px solid #ccc;
  border-radius: 5px;
  text-align: left;
}

.add-task-form {
  display: flex;
  margin-bottom: 15px;
}

.add-task-form input {
  flex-grow: 1;
  padding: 8px;
  border: 1px solid #ccc;
  border-radius: 4px;
  margin-right: 10px;
}

.add-task-form button {
  background-color: #007bff;
  color: #fff;
  padding: 8px 15px;
  border: none;
  border-radius: 4px;
  cursor: pointer;
}

ul {
  list-style-type: none; /* Remove bullet points */
```

```
    padding: 0;
}

button {
    background-color: #dc3545; /* Red color for delete and
clear */
    color: #fff;
    padding: 8px 15px;
    border: none;
    border-radius: 4px;
    cursor: pointer;
    margin-top: 10px;
}
```

Explanation:

- o max-width, margin, padding, border, border-radius, text-align: These properties are used to style the container and provide a clean and organized layout.
- o display: flex, flex-grow, margin-right: These properties are used to style the add task form and ensure that the input field and button are properly aligned.
- o background-color, color, padding, border, border-radius, cursor: These properties are used to style the buttons and make them visually appealing.
- o list-style-type: none, padding: 0: These properties are used to remove the default bullet points from the unordered list and remove the default padding.

2. **Styling the TodoItemComponent:**
   - o **List Item:** We'll add styling to the <li> element to provide spacing and a bottom border.
   - o **Completed Task:** We'll add styling to the completed class to visually indicate that a task has been completed (e.g., by striking through the text).
   - o **Checkbox:** (Optional) We'll add styling to the checkbox to make it more visually appealing.

```
    /* todo-item.component.css */
li {
    display: flex;
    align-items: center;
    padding: 8px;
    border-bottom: 1px solid #eee;
}
```

```
li:last-child {
  border-bottom: none;
}

li input[type="checkbox"] {
  margin-right: 10px;
}

li.completed span {
  text-decoration: line-through; /* Strike-through completed
tasks */
  color: #aaa; /* Muted color for completed tasks */
}
```

Explanation:

- o display: flex, align-items, padding, border-bottom: These properties are used to style the list items and provide a consistent layout.
- o li:last-child: This selector removes the bottom border from the last list item.
- o margin-right: This property adds spacing between the checkbox and the task description.
- o text-decoration: line-through, color: These properties are used to style completed tasks and visually indicate their completion status.

Beyond Basic CSS: Enhancing the Styling

Here are some ideas for enhancing the styling of your to-do list app:

- **Use a CSS Framework:** Consider using a CSS framework such as Bootstrap or Materialize to quickly and easily create a visually appealing and responsive user interface.
- **Use CSS Preprocessors:** Use a CSS preprocessor such as Sass or Less to write more maintainable and organized CSS code.
- **Implement a Theme:** Allow the user to choose from different themes to customize the appearance of the application.
- **Use CSS Animations and Transitions:** Add CSS animations and transitions to create a more engaging and interactive user experience.

Personal Insight: I've found that spending time on styling is just as important as spending time on functionality. A well-styled application is more likely to be used and appreciated by users.

A Note on Accessibility:

When styling your application, it's important to consider accessibility. Make sure that your color choices provide sufficient contrast, that your font sizes are large enough to be readable, and that your application is navigable using keyboard only.

Conclusion: A Polished Masterpiece

By adding these final touches of styling, we've transformed our to-do list app from a functional prototype into a visually appealing and user-friendly application. Remember that styling is not just about aesthetics; it's about enhancing usability and creating a positive user experience. You are now an application stylist! With styling complete, you have a fully functional and presentable to-do list application!

Chapter 11: Next Steps in Angular - Expanding Your Horizons

Congratulations! You've made it to the end of this introductory guide to Angular. You've learned a lot about the core concepts, how to build components, and how to create interactive user interfaces. But this is just the beginning! The world of Angular is vast and ever-evolving, and there's always more to learn. This chapter will serve as your launchpad, providing a glimpse into the exciting areas you can explore to take your Angular skills to the next level.

Beyond the Fundamentals: A Journey of Continuous Learning

Think of this chapter as your compass, pointing you towards new and exciting destinations in your Angular journey. We'll cover some key concepts conceptually, giving you a taste of what's to come, and provide resources to help you continue learning.

11.1 Introduction to Services and Dependency Injection (Conceptual): The Power of Reusable Logic

We've already built a functional to-do list app, but as applications grow in complexity, managing logic within individual components can become unwieldy. Think of Services and Dependency Injection (DI) as the organizational principles that enable you to build maintainable, scalable, and testable Angular applications. This section is your introduction to these powerful concepts.

Beyond Components: Extracting and Centralizing Logic

While components are responsible for the user interface and presentation, services are designed to encapsulate reusable logic and data access. They help to keep your components lean and focused, making them easier to understand and maintain. Think of services as specialists, handling specific tasks and freeing up your components to focus on their core responsibilities.

Why Use Services?

- **Code Reusability:** Services allow you to share logic across multiple components, avoiding code duplication and promoting consistency.
- **Separation of Concerns:** Services enforce a clear separation of concerns, making your code more modular and easier to understand.
- **Testability:** Services are easier to test because they are self-contained and have well-defined interfaces.
- **Maintainability:** Services make your code easier to maintain by centralizing common logic in a single place. Changes to the logic only need to be made in the service, rather than in multiple components.
- **State Management:** Services can be used to manage application state, providing a centralized location for storing and updating data.

Dependency Injection: Making Services Accessible

So, how do components access these services? This is where dependency injection (DI) comes in. Dependency injection is a design pattern that allows you to inject dependencies (services) into components and other services. This means that instead of creating the dependencies themselves, the components and services receive them from an external source (the Angular injector).

The Key Benefits of Dependency Injection:

- **Loose Coupling:** DI reduces the coupling between components and their dependencies, making your code more flexible and easier to change. Components don't need to know how to create their dependencies; they simply receive them from the injector.
- **Testability:** DI makes it easier to test components by allowing you to inject mock dependencies. This allows you to test the component in isolation, without having to rely on real dependencies. Mocked services help create predictable tests.
- **Reusability:** DI makes it easier to reuse components and services in different parts of your application. You can simply inject the dependencies they need, without having to modify their code.

Conceptualizing Dependency Injection

Imagine a car factory. The car needs various components, such as an engine, wheels, and a steering wheel. Instead of the car factory building these components itself, it receives them from external suppliers (the dependencies). Dependency injection is like the system that manages the delivery of these components to the car factory, ensuring that they are available when needed.

The Angular Injector: Managing Dependencies

Angular has a built-in dependency injection system that automatically manages the creation and delivery of dependencies. The injector is responsible for:

1. **Creating Instances of Services:** When a component or service requests a dependency, the injector checks if it has already created an instance of that dependency. If not, it creates a new instance.
2. **Resolving Dependencies:** The injector resolves any dependencies that the service itself has. This means that if the service needs other services, the injector will create those services as well.
3. **Injecting Dependencies:** The injector injects the dependencies into the component or service, making them available for use.

Providing Services:

To make a service available for dependency injection, you need to "provide" it. This tells Angular how to create an instance of the service. There are several ways to provide services in Angular:

- **providedIn: 'root':** This is the most common way to provide services. It tells Angular to create a single instance of the service that is available throughout the entire application. This is ideal for services that manage global application state or provide utility functions.

```
import { Injectable } from '@angular/core';

@Injectable({
  providedIn: 'root' // Makes the service available globally
})
export class MyService {
  // ...
}
```

- **Providing in a Module:** You can also provide services in a specific module. This makes the service available only to components within

189

that module. This is useful for services that are specific to a particular feature.
- **Providing in a Component:** Finally, you can provide services in a specific component. This makes the service available only to that component and its child components. This is useful for services that are specific to a particular component and should not be shared with other parts of the application.

Personal Insight: Understanding services and dependency injection is crucial for building scalable and maintainable Angular applications. It took me some time to fully grasp these concepts, but once I did, it completely transformed the way I wrote Angular code.

A Glimpse into the Future: Exploring Services and Dependency Injection in Detail

In a later, more advanced section, we'll dive deeper into services and dependency injection, exploring:

- **Creating custom services.**
- **Using different injection tokens.**
- **Understanding the scope of providers.**
- **Testing services with dependency injection.**

Conclusion: Building a Robust and Modular Application

Services and dependency injection are fundamental concepts that enable you to build robust, modular, and testable Angular applications. By mastering these techniques, you can create applications that are easy to understand, maintain, and scale. You have now learned to build a strong and scalable foundation!

11.2 Introduction to Angular Routing: Mapping the User's Journey

We've built components, wired them up with data, and styled their appearance. But what about *navigation*? How do we allow users to move between different views within our single-page application (SPA)? This is where Angular Routing comes into play. Think of Angular Routing as your application's internal GPS, guiding users seamlessly between different parts of your application without full page reloads.

Beyond Single Pages: Creating Multi-View Experiences

While the term "single-page application" implies that there's only one HTML page, that doesn't mean that your application can't have multiple views or sections. Angular Routing allows you to create the *illusion* of multiple pages by dynamically updating the content of the main page based on the current URL.

Why Use Angular Routing?

- **SPA Navigation:** Enables navigation between different views within a single-page application, providing a smoother and more responsive user experience.
- **Bookmarkable URLs:** Allows users to bookmark specific views in your application, making it easy to return to them later.
- **Search Engine Optimization (SEO):** Although SPAs can be challenging for SEO, Angular Routing can help improve your application's SEO by creating unique and crawlable URLs for each view.
- **Improved User Experience:** By avoiding full page reloads, Angular Routing can significantly improve the user experience, making your application feel more like a native app.
- **Organization of Features:** Routing naturally structures application features.

The Key Concepts: Routes, Router Outlet, and Router Links

Angular Routing revolves around three core concepts:

- **Routes:** Routes are definitions that specify the mapping between URLs and components. Each route defines which component should be displayed when the user navigates to a specific URL.
- **Router Outlet:** The <router-outlet> directive acts as a placeholder in your application's template. Angular will dynamically render the component associated with the current route inside this element. Think of it as the stage where different "acts" (components) perform.
- **Router Links:** The routerLink directive creates navigation links that allow users to navigate between different routes. When the user clicks on a router link, Angular updates the URL and displays the corresponding component in the router outlet. These are the navigation arrows for the user.

Conceptual Example: A Simple Website with Three Pages

Imagine you're building a simple website with three pages: a home page, an about page, and a contact page. You can use Angular Routing to define the following routes:

```
import { Routes } from '@angular/router';
import { HomeComponent } from './home/home.component';
import { AboutComponent } from './about/about.component';
import { ContactComponent } from
'./contact/contact.component';

const routes: Routes = [
  { path: 'home', component: HomeComponent },
  { path: 'about', component: AboutComponent },
  { path: 'contact', component: ContactComponent },
  { path: '', redirectTo: '/home', pathMatch: 'full' }, //
Default route
  { path: '**', redirectTo: '/home' } // Wildcard route
];
```

Explanation:

- { path: 'home', component: HomeComponent }: This route specifies that when the user navigates to the /home URL, the HomeComponent should be displayed.
- { path: 'about', component: AboutComponent }: This route specifies that when the user navigates to the /about URL, the AboutComponent should be displayed.
- { path: 'contact', component: ContactComponent }: This route specifies that when the user navigates to the /contact URL, the ContactComponent should be displayed.
- { path: '', redirectTo: '/home', pathMatch: 'full' }: This route specifies that when the user navigates to the root URL (/), they should be redirected to the /home URL. The pathMatch: 'full' option ensures that the redirect only occurs when the entire URL matches the specified path.
- { path: '**', redirectTo: '/home' }: This is a wildcard route. It matches any URL that doesn't match any of the other routes in the configuration. This is often used to redirect users to a "404 Not Found" page or a default route (as we're doing here).

Putting It Together: A Seamless Navigation Experience

To create a seamless navigation experience, you would add the <router-outlet> directive to your application template:

```html
<!-- app.component.html -->
<nav>
  <a routerLink="/home">Home</a>
  <a routerLink="/about">About</a>
  <a routerLink="/contact">Contact</a>
</nav>

<router-outlet></router-outlet>
```

This code will display a navigation menu with links to the home, about, and contact pages. When the user clicks on one of these links, Angular will update the URL and display the corresponding component in the <router-outlet>.

Beyond the Basics: Advanced Routing Concepts

Angular Routing offers a wide range of advanced features, including:

- **Route Parameters:** Passing data to components through the URL. This is useful for displaying details about a specific item (e.g., /products/123 to display details about product with ID 123).
- **Child Routes:** Creating nested routes for complex application structures.
- **Lazy Loading:** Loading modules and components on demand, improving the initial load time of your application. This is critical for large applications.
- **Route Guards:** Protecting routes by implementing authentication and authorization checks.

Personal Insight: Angular Routing transformed the way I built web applications. Before, I was manually managing navigation using JavaScript, which was tedious and error-prone. Angular Routing provides a clean, structured, and powerful way to create single-page applications with multiple views.

A Glimpse into the Future: Exploring Angular Routing in Detail

In a later, more advanced section, we'll dive deeper into Angular Routing, exploring:

- Implementing route parameters.
- Creating child routes.
- Using route guards to protect routes.
- Implementing lazy loading to improve performance.

Conclusion: Navigating the SPA Landscape

Angular Routing is an essential tool for building single-page applications with multiple views. By mastering the concepts of routes, router outlets, and router links, you can create seamless and engaging navigation experiences for your users. You are now ready to guide your users through the world you create!

11.3 Introduction to HTTP Communication: Connecting Your App to the Data Universe

We've learned how to structure our application, display data, and navigate between views. Now, let's explore how to connect our application to the outside world by fetching data from and sending data to backend servers. Think of HTTP communication as your application's lifeline to the data universe, allowing it to interact with APIs and access the information it needs to function.

Beyond Local Data: Accessing the Power of External APIs

Modern web applications rarely rely solely on data that is stored locally. They often need to communicate with backend servers to fetch data from databases, save user information, authenticate users, and perform other operations. HTTP communication provides the standard mechanism for exchanging data between your Angular application and these backend servers.

Why is HTTP Communication So Important?

- **Data Retrieval:** Allows your application to fetch dynamic data from backend APIs to display to the user. This enables you to create applications that are always up-to-date with the latest information.
- **Data Persistence:** Allows your application to save data to backend databases, ensuring that the data is stored securely and can be accessed by other users.

- **Authentication and Authorization:** Enables your application to authenticate users and authorize them to access specific resources, ensuring that only authorized users can access sensitive data.
- **Integration with Third-Party Services:** Allows your application to integrate with third-party services, such as social media platforms, payment gateways, and mapping services.
- **Decoupling Frontend and Backend:** Provides a clear separation between the frontend (Angular application) and the backend (server-side logic and database). This makes it easier to develop, test, and maintain your application.

The Key Concepts: Requests, Responses, and Observables

HTTP communication in Angular revolves around three core concepts:

- **Requests:** An HTTP request is a message sent from your Angular application to a backend server. The request specifies what data you want to fetch, what action you want to perform, or what data you want to send to the server.
- **Responses:** An HTTP response is a message sent back from the backend server to your Angular application. The response contains the data that you requested, the status of the request, and any other relevant information.
- **Observables:** In Angular, HTTP requests are handled using Observables from the RxJS library. An Observable represents a stream of data that can be emitted over time. In the case of HTTP requests, the Observable emits the response data when it's received from the server.

Conceptual Analogy: Ordering Food at a Restaurant

Imagine you're ordering food at a restaurant:

- **HTTP Request:** Your order to the waiter specifying what you want to eat. This would include the type of request (GET, POST, PUT, DELETE), the URL of the resource you want, and any data you want to send to the server (e.g., your order details).
- **HTTP Response:** The food delivered to your table by the waiter. This includes the data (the food), a status code (e.g., 200 OK, 404 Not Found), and any other relevant information (e.g., cooking time).
- **Observable:** The entire process of waiting for your food to be prepared and delivered. You don't get the food immediately; you

have to wait for it to be prepared and delivered. The Observable represents this waiting process.

Common HTTP Methods:

- **GET:** Used to retrieve data from a server.
- **POST:** Used to create new data on a server.
- **PUT:** Used to update existing data on a server.
- **DELETE:** Used to delete data from a server.

The HttpClient Service: Your Gateway to the Backend

Angular provides the HttpClient service to make HTTP requests. This service is part of the @angular/common/http module and provides methods for making GET, POST, PUT, DELETE, and other types of HTTP requests.

Using Observables for Asynchronous Operations:

HTTP requests are asynchronous operations, meaning that they don't block the main thread of your application. This allows your application to remain responsive while waiting for the server to respond.

To handle asynchronous operations, Angular uses Observables from the RxJS library. An Observable represents a stream of data that can be emitted over time. You can subscribe to an Observable to receive the data emitted by the Observable, and you can use RxJS operators to transform and manipulate the data stream.

Personal Insight: I initially found Observables a bit confusing, but once I understood their power for handling asynchronous operations, they became an indispensable tool in my Angular development workflow.

A Glimpse into the Future: Exploring HTTP Communication in Detail

In a later, more advanced section, we'll dive deeper into HTTP communication, exploring:

- Making different types of HTTP requests (GET, POST, PUT, DELETE).
- Setting request headers.
- Handling response data.
- Handling errors.

- Using RxJS operators to transform and manipulate data streams.
- Implementing authentication and authorization.

Conclusion: Connecting Your Application to the World

HTTP communication is an essential skill for building modern web applications. By mastering HTTP communication, you can connect your Angular application to the outside world, fetching data from backend servers, saving user information, and integrating with third-party services. You now know the route to a full-stack application!

11.4 Further Learning Resources: Equipping You for Continued Growth

You've completed this introductory journey into the world of Angular! But remember, this is just the beginning. The field of web development, and Angular in particular, is constantly evolving, with new features, best practices, and tools emerging all the time. Think of this section as equipping you with a compass, map, and survival kit for your continued exploration of the Angular landscape.

Beyond This Book: Embracing a Culture of Continuous Learning

Staying up-to-date is essential for any software developer, and it's especially important in the rapidly changing world of web development. The resources listed below will help you continue to learn and grow as an Angular developer.

Key Resources for Angular Mastery:

- **Official Angular Documentation: The Definitive Guide**
  - **URL:** https://angular.io/docs
  - **Description:** The official Angular documentation is the single best resource for learning about Angular. It provides comprehensive guides, tutorials, and API documentation. It's well-organized, up-to-date, and covers everything from the basics to advanced topics.

    Expert Commentary: The Angular documentation is often the first place I go when I have a question about Angular. It's generally accurate and provides detailed explanations of complex concepts.

Always prioritize the official documentation as your primary source of truth.

- **Official Angular Blog: Staying Up-to-Date**
  - **URL:** https://blog.angular.io/
  - **Description:** The official Angular blog provides updates on the latest Angular features, releases, and best practices. It's a great way to stay informed about the latest developments in the Angular ecosystem.

Expert Commentary: The Angular blog is a must-read for any serious Angular developer. It's where the Angular team announces new features, provides insights into the design decisions behind the framework, and shares tips for writing better Angular code.

- **Angular University: Structured Learning Paths**
  - **URL:** https://angular-university.io/
  - **Description:** Angular University offers high-quality Angular courses and tutorials that cover a wide range of topics. They provide structured learning paths that are designed to help you master Angular from beginner to advanced.

Expert Commentary: Angular University is a great resource for developers who prefer a more structured learning approach. Their courses are well-produced, comprehensive, and cover a wide range of topics.

- **Stack Overflow: Your Community Lifeline**
  - **URL:** https://stackoverflow.com/questions/tagged/angular
  - **Description:** Stack Overflow is a question-and-answer website that is a valuable resource for developers of all skill levels. The Angular tag on Stack Overflow is a great place to ask questions and get help from the Angular community.

Expert Commentary: Stack Overflow is an invaluable resource for troubleshooting issues and finding solutions to common problems. When asking questions on Stack Overflow, be sure to provide clear and concise details about your problem, including the code you're using and any error messages you're seeing.

- **GitHub: Exploring the Open Source Universe**

- o **URL:** https://github.com/topics/angular (or search for "angular")
- o **Description:** GitHub is a code hosting platform where you can find a vast collection of open-source Angular projects. Exploring these projects can be a great way to learn from other developers and contribute to the community.

Expert Commentary: GitHub is a goldmine of information for Angular developers. You can find everything from small example projects to large-scale enterprise applications. Studying the code in these projects can help you learn new techniques, discover best practices, and improve your understanding of Angular.

- **Online Course Platforms: Udemy, Coursera, Pluralsight and More**
  - o **Description:** These platforms offer a plethora of Angular courses, ranging from beginner-friendly introductions to advanced deep dives.
  - o **Recommendation:** It's best to research the instructors carefully, read reviews, and choose courses that are consistently well-rated. Look for courses that are regularly updated to reflect the latest Angular versions and best practices.
- **Medium and Dev.to: Community Knowledge and Insights**
  - o **Description:** These publishing platforms are home to a vast collection of articles, tutorials, and opinion pieces written by Angular developers from around the world.
  - o **Recommendation:** Use keyword searches within these platforms to find content on specific Angular topics. Be aware that the quality can vary significantly, so critically evaluate the information you find and cross-reference it with other reliable sources.

Personal Insight: I've learned so much from the Angular community over the years. Don't be afraid to ask questions, share your knowledge, and contribute to open-source projects. It's a great way to learn and grow as a developer.

A Note on Staying Current:

Angular is a rapidly evolving framework, and new versions are released regularly. It's important to stay up-to-date with the latest features and best practices to ensure that your skills remain relevant. Make it a habit to check the Angular blog and documentation regularly.

Conclusion: A Lifetime of Learning

This section has provided you with a set of valuable resources to help you continue your Angular journey. Remember that learning Angular is a continuous process, and there's always more to discover. Embrace a culture of continuous learning, and you'll be well-equipped to thrive in the exciting and ever-changing world of web development! You now have the map and tools necessary to continue your exploration.

11.5 Best Practices for Beginners: Navigating the Angular Landscape with Confidence

You've learned the fundamentals of Angular, built a to-do list app, and explored various resources for continued learning. Now, let's equip you with some essential best practices to help you navigate the Angular landscape with confidence and avoid common pitfalls. Think of these as guiding principles that will steer you towards writing cleaner, more maintainable, and more efficient Angular code.

Beyond Code: Cultivating Good Development Habits

Learning a framework is only part of the equation. Cultivating good development habits and following best practices is crucial for becoming a skilled and effective Angular developer. These practices will help you write code that is easier to understand, test, maintain, and scale.

Key Best Practices for Angular Beginners:

- **Embrace the Official Angular Style Guide: Your North Star**
  - **URL:** https://angular.io/guide/styleguide
  - **Description:** The official Angular Style Guide is a set of recommendations and best practices for writing Angular code. It covers everything from naming conventions to code formatting to architectural patterns.

  Expert Commentary: The Angular Style Guide is your North Star. Following it consistently will make your code more readable, maintainable, and easier to collaborate on. It provides a common language for Angular developers and promotes consistency across projects. Make it your habit to consult the style guide regularly.

- **Master TypeScript: Angular's Partner in Crime**
  - **Description:** Angular is built with TypeScript, a superset of JavaScript that adds static typing and other features. Using TypeScript is highly recommended for Angular development, as it helps you catch errors early and makes your code more maintainable.

Expert Commentary: Learning TypeScript is an investment that will pay off handsomely. It's not just about adding types; it's about writing more robust, reliable, and scalable code. Embrace TypeScript, and it will become your superpower. If you have never used a "typed" language, this is a must, even if you hate it at first. Persist, and you'll soon appreciate TypeScript.

- **Write Unit Tests: Your Safety Net**
  - **Description:** Unit tests are small, automated tests that verify the behavior of individual components, services, and pipes. Writing unit tests is an essential part of Angular development, as it helps you catch bugs early and ensures that your code is working correctly.

Expert Commentary: Testing can feel like a chore at first, but it's an invaluable practice. Think of unit tests as your safety net, protecting you from unexpected errors and regressions. Writing tests will also force you to think more carefully about the design of your code, leading to better overall code quality. Aim for high test coverage.

- **Embrace the Angular CLI: Your Productivity Multiplier**
  - **Description:** The Angular CLI is a powerful command-line tool that automates many common tasks in Angular development, such as creating new projects, generating components, running tests, and building your application for production.

Expert Commentary: The Angular CLI is your productivity multiplier. Learn to use it effectively, and you'll be able to develop Angular applications much faster and with fewer errors. Resist the urge to manually create files and folders; let the CLI do the heavy lifting. Embrace the CLI and you'll thank yourself later.

- **Stay Up-to-Date: The Ever-Evolving Landscape**
  - **Description:** Angular is constantly evolving, with new versions being released regularly. It's important to stay up-to-date with the latest features and best practices to ensure that your skills remain relevant.

Expert Commentary: Make it a habit to check the Angular blog and documentation regularly for updates and announcements. Follow Angular experts on social media and attend Angular conferences and meetups to learn from others in the community. The Angular world is constantly changing, so stay curious and keep learning.

- **Start Small, Build Incrementally: The Power of Iteration**
  - **Description:** Don't try to learn everything at once. Start with the basics and gradually work your way up to more advanced topics. Build small, focused applications to practice your skills and solidify your understanding.

Expert Commentary: The best way to learn Angular is by doing. Start with a small project and gradually add more features and complexity as you become more comfortable with the framework. Don't be afraid to experiment and try new things. It's how you learn and grow. Think of each project as a stepping stone on your path to mastery.

- **Master the Fundamentals:**
  - **Description:** Focus on understanding the core concepts of Angular, such as components, directives, pipes, services, dependency injection, and data binding. A solid foundation in these concepts will make it easier to learn more advanced topics later on.

Expert Commentary: Don't be tempted to skip ahead to advanced topics before you have a solid understanding of the fundamentals. A strong foundation is essential for building complex and scalable applications.

- **Ask Questions and Seek Help:**
  - **Description:** Don't be afraid to ask questions when you get stuck. The Angular community is large and supportive, and there are many resources available to help you.

Expert Commentary: There's no shame in asking for help. Everyone gets stuck from time to time. Reach out to the Angular community on Stack Overflow, online forums, or social media. You'll be surprised at how willing people are to help.

- **Be Patient and Persistent:**
  - **Description:** Learning Angular takes time and effort. Don't get discouraged if you don't understand everything right away. Be patient with yourself and keep practicing.

Expert Commentary: Learning Angular is a marathon, not a sprint. There will be times when you feel overwhelmed or frustrated, but don't give up. Keep practicing, keep learning, and eventually, you'll reach your goals. Persistence is key.

- **Learn to Debug Effectively**
  - **Description**: When something goes wrong, it's essential to effectively use your browser's developer tools and console to track down what's happening. Learn how to set breakpoints, inspect variables, and read stack traces.

Expert Commentary: Mastering the debugger is like having X-ray vision for your code. It transforms the process of troubleshooting from guesswork to methodical investigation. This is an indispensable skill.

Personal Insight: I made many mistakes when I first started learning Angular, but I learned from those mistakes and eventually became a skilled Angular developer. Don't be afraid to make mistakes; it's part of the learning process.

Conclusion: Embarking on a Path of Mastery

This section has provided you with a set of essential best practices to help you navigate the Angular landscape with confidence and avoid common pitfalls. By following these guidelines, you'll be well-equipped to write cleaner, more maintainable, and more efficient Angular code. You now have the tools and knowledge to embark on a path of continuous learning and become a true Angular expert! Keep learning, keep building, and most importantly, keep having fun!

Appendix: Your Reference and Troubleshooting Guide

Congratulations on reaching the end of this Angular journey! While you've covered a lot of ground, the learning doesn't stop here. Think of this appendix as your survival kit and quick-reference guide, providing essential information to help you navigate common challenges and continue your Angular development.

A Quick Note on Style: While the rest of this book maintains a conversational tone, the Appendix is all about reference material. You'll find short and to-the-point explanations.

Glossary of Terms: Deciphering the Jargon

Angular, like any technology, has its own vocabulary. This glossary defines some of the most common terms you'll encounter, helping you to understand the language of Angular development.

- **Angular CLI:** Command Line Interface. A tool for scaffolding, building, testing, and deploying Angular applications.
- **Component:** A self-contained UI element that encapsulates its own logic, template, and styling.
- **Data Binding:** The process of connecting data in your component to the HTML template.
- **Directive:** A marker on a DOM element that instructs Angular to modify its behavior or appearance.
- **Dependency Injection (DI):** A design pattern that allows you to inject dependencies into components and services.
- **EventEmitter:** A class that allows components to emit custom events to their parent components.
- **FormsModule:** The Angular module that provides directives and services for working with template-driven forms.
- **HTTP:** Hypertext Transfer Protocol. The protocol used for communication between web browsers and servers.
- **Interpolation:** A data binding technique that displays data in the template using double curly braces {{ }}.
- **NgModule:** A decorator that marks a class as an Angular module.
- **Node.js:** A JavaScript runtime environment that allows you to run JavaScript code outside of a web browser.

- **npm:** Node Package Manager. A package manager for JavaScript that is used to install and manage dependencies for your Angular project.
- **Observable:** A type from the RxJS library that represents a stream of data over time.
- **Pipe:** A function that transforms data before it is displayed in the template.
- **Property Binding:** A data binding technique that sets the properties of HTML elements to values from your component.
- **Reactive Forms:** An Angular form handling approach that uses a more programmatic setup within the component class.
- **Route:** A mapping between a URL and a component.
- **RouterModule:** The Angular module that provides routing functionality.
- RouterLink: A directive used in a template to create a link to a specific route.
- RouterOutlet: A directive in a template that marks where the content of a routed component will be displayed.
- **RxJS:** Reactive Extensions for JavaScript. A library for working with asynchronous data streams and events.
- **Service:** A class that encapsulates reusable logic and data access.
- **SPA:** Single-Page Application. A web application that loads a single HTML page and dynamically updates the content using JavaScript.
- **Template-Driven Forms:** An Angular form handling approach that primarily uses directives in the template to manage the form.
- **TypeScript:** A superset of JavaScript that adds static typing and other features.
- [(ngModel)]: A directive that creates two-way data binding between form element and a property in your class.

Common Errors and Troubleshooting: Your Rescue Kit

Encountering errors is an inevitable part of the development process. This section provides guidance on troubleshooting common Angular errors and resolving common problems.

- **"Cannot read property '...' of undefined"**:
  - **Cause:** This error typically occurs when you're trying to access a property of an object that is null or undefined.
  - **Solution:** Make sure the object exists and is properly initialized before accessing its properties. Use the safe navigation operator (?.) to prevent this error.

- **"NG0100: Expression has changed after it was checked"**:
  - o **Cause:** This error occurs when Angular detects a change in a component's data during the change detection cycle.
  - o **Solution:** This is often caused by updating data in a lifecycle hook (like ngAfterViewInit). Consider using setTimeout or ChangeDetectorRef.detectChanges() cautiously to address this. Be mindful of what changes trigger the cycle.
- **"No provider for ... "**:
  - o **Cause:** This error occurs when Angular cannot find a provider for a dependency that is being injected into a component or service.
  - o **Solution:** Make sure the service is properly decorated with @Injectable() and is provided in a module or component using the providers array.
- **"Template parse errors: Can't bind to '...' since it isn't a known property of '...'."**:
  - o **Cause:** This error occurs when you're trying to bind to a property of an HTML element that doesn't exist or that is misspelled.
  - o **Solution:** Double-check the spelling of the property name and make sure that the property is actually a valid property of the element. Also, check that you've imported any necessary modules for custom elements.
- **"Module not found: Error: Can't resolve '...' "**:
  - o **Cause:** This error occurs when Angular cannot find a module that you're trying to import.
  - o **Solution:** Make sure the module is installed correctly (using npm install) and that the import path is correct.
- **CORS (Cross-Origin Resource Sharing) Issues:**
  - o **Cause:** These arise when your Angular application (running on one domain) tries to make HTTP requests to a backend API hosted on a different domain, and the server does not allow this.
  - o **Solution:** The backend server must be configured to allow cross-origin requests from your Angular application's domain. This is typically done by setting appropriate headers in the server's response. In development, you can sometimes use a proxy server to circumvent CORS restrictions.
- **My changes aren't showing up!**:
  - o **Cause:** Often caching, incorrect saves, or missed ng serve triggers

○ **Solution**: Triple-check that your changes have been saved in your editor and that the ng serve process is running and compiling the code correctly. If the issue persists, try clearing your browser cache or restarting the ng serve process.

Helpful Resources and Links: Your Toolkit for Success

This section provides a curated list of helpful resources and links to help you continue learning Angular.

- **Official Angular Documentation:** https://angular.io/docs - The official Angular documentation is the best source of information about Angular.
- **Angular CLI Documentation:** https://angular.io/cli - Learn how to use the Angular CLI to create, build, test, and deploy your Angular applications.
- **RxJS Documentation:** https://rxjs.dev/ - RxJS is a library for working with asynchronous data streams and events. Angular makes heavy use of RxJS.
- **TypeScript Documentation:** https://www.typescriptlang.org/docs/ - Learn more about TypeScript, the language used to build Angular applications.
- **Angular Material:** https://material.angular.io/ - A component library providing pre-built UI components following the Material Design specification.
- **PrimeNG:** https://www.primefaces.org/primeng/ - A comprehensive suite of UI components for Angular.
- **NG-Bootstrap:** https://ng-bootstrap.github.io/ - A library providing Bootstrap components for Angular.
- **Stack Overflow Angular Tag:** https://stackoverflow.com/questions/tagged/angular - A great place to ask questions and get help from the Angular community.

Personal Insight: I've found that keeping a running list of common errors and their solutions can be incredibly helpful. Whenever I encounter a new error, I add it to my list along with the steps I took to resolve it. This helps me to quickly troubleshoot similar issues in the future.

Conclusion: Your Toolkit for the Journey Ahead

This appendix is designed to be your companion as you continue your Angular journey. Use the glossary to understand unfamiliar terms, consult the troubleshooting guide when you encounter errors, and leverage the helpful resources and links to expand your knowledge and skills. You've got this! Now go forth and build amazing Angular applications!